Top 25 locator map
(continues on inside
back cover)

◄

# CityPack
# **Edinburgh** *Top 25*

If you have any comments
or suggestions for this guide
you can contact the editor at
*Citypack@TheAA.com*

**AA Publishing**
Find out more about AA Publishing and the wide range
of travel publications and services the AA provides by
visiting our website at *www.TheAA.com/bookshop*

# About This Book

## KEY TO SYMBOLS

➕ Map reference to the accompanying fold-out map and Top 25 locator map

✉ Address

☎ Telephone number

🕐 Opening/closing times

🍴 Restaurant or café on premises or nearby

🚉 Nearest railway station

🚌 Nearest bus route

🚢 Nearest riverboat or ferry stop

♿ Facilities for visitors with disabilities

✋ Admission charges: Expensive (over £6), Moderate (£3–£6) and Inexpensive (under £3)

↔ Other nearby places of interest

❓ Other practical information

▶ Indicates the page where you will find a fuller description

ℹ Tourist information

## ORGANIZATION

This guide is divided into six chapters:
- Planning Ahead, Getting There
- Living Edinburgh—Edinburgh Now, Edinburgh Then, Time to Shop, Out and About, Walks, Edinburgh by Night
- Edinburgh's Top 25 Sights
- Edinburgh's Best—best of the rest
- Where To—detailed listings of restaurants, hotels, shops and nightlife
- Travel Facts—practical information

In addition, easy-to-read side panels provide extra facts and snippets, highlights of places to visit and invaluable practical advice.

The colours of the tabs on the page corners match the colours of the triangles aligned with the chapter names on the contents page opposite.

## MAPS

**The fold-out map** in the wallet at the back of this book is a comprehensive street plan of Edinburgh. The first (or only) grid reference given for each attraction refers to this map. **The Top 25 locator map** found on the inside front and back covers of the book itself is for quick reference. It shows the Top 25 Sights, described on pages 26–50, which are clearly plotted by number (**1**–**25**, not page number) across the city. The second map reference given for the Top 25 Sights refers to this map.

# Contents

# Planning Ahead

## WHEN TO GO

Edinburgh lies on the eastern side of Scotland, which is cooler, windier and drier than the west. The occasional outbreak of *haar* (sea mist) along the coast will shroud the city in thick mist. At any time of year you are likely to meet rain, but the chances are it will not last for long. Many tourist sites close in winter, but major city museums stay open year round.

### TIME

Scotland is on GMT (Greenwich Mean Time), but switches to British Summer Time (1 hour ahead) from late March to late October.

### AVERAGE DAILY MAXIMUM TEMPERATURES

| JAN | FEB | MAR | APR | MAY | JUN | JUL | AUG | SEP | OCT | NOV | DEC |
|-----|-----|-----|-----|-----|-----|-----|-----|-----|-----|-----|-----|
| 39°F | 39°F | 43°F | 48°F | 54°F | 61°F | 63°F | 61°F | 59°F | 54°F | 45°F | 41°F |
| 4°C | 4°C | 6°C | 9°C | 12°C | 16°C | 17°C | 16°C | 15°C | 12°C | 7°C | 5°C |

**Spring** (March to May) has the best chance of clear skies and sunny days.
**Summer** (June to August) is unpredictable—it may be hot and sunny, but it can also be cloudy and wet.
**Autumn** (September to November) is usually more settled and there's a good chance of fine weather, but nothing is guaranteed.
**Winter** (December to February) can be cold, dark, wet and dreary, but there are also sparkling, clear, sunny days of frost, when the light is brilliant.

## WHAT'S ON

**January** *Burns Night* (25 Jan): the birthday of the city's national poet, celebrated throughout with haggis and whisky.
**April** *Edinburgh Science Festival*: science and technology events at various venues.
*Easter Festival*: Over 4,000 people gather in the city on Easter Sunday to celebrate cultural diversity, youth, happiness and heritage.
*Ceilidh Culture*: events centred around traditional Scottish arts.
**May** *Scottish International*

*Children's Festival*: Britain's largest performing arts festival for young people.
**June** *Royal Highland Show*: (► 62).
*Edinburgh Marathon*.
**July/August** *Edinburgh International Jazz & Blues Festival*: ten days of jazz performed by big names and new talent.
**August** *Edinburgh International Festival*: over three weeks, some of the world's best theatre, opera, music and dance.
*Edinburgh Festival Fringe*: (► 62).

*Edinburgh Military Tattoo*: (► 62).
*Edinburgh International Film Festival*: one of the most respected film festivals in the world (► 82).
*International Book Festival*: occupies a tented village in Charlotte Square.
**September** *Mela*: a vibrant celebration of cultural diversity with music, dance and street performers.
**November/December** *Capital Christmas*: (► 62).
**December/January** *Edinburgh Hogmanay*: (► 62).

## EDINBURGH ONLINE

**www.edinburgh.org**
Edinburgh's official website for tourists has up-to-date comprehensive information on city attractions, events, guided tours, shopping, accommodation, eating out and lots more.

**www.visitscotland.com**
The official Scotland Tourist Board website, with a comprehensive database of information covering everything from weather, transport and events to shopping, nightlife and accommodation throughout Scotland.

**www.eventful-edinburgh.com**
All the information you need to know about what to see and do in Edinburgh, and the best places to stay to suit all budgets.

**www.edinburghguide.com**
An informative guide to attractions, entertainment, recreation, eating out and accommodation, plus links to other sites.

**www.nms.ac.uk**
The National Museum of Scotland looks after many of Scotland's important museum collections. Its website provides detailed information about the museums in its care, including most of the major ones in Edinburgh.

**www.undiscoveredscotland.co.uk**
An online guide to Scotland. The Edinburgh section has many useful links to other good sources of information.

**www.nts.org.uk**
The National Trust for Scotland looks after buildings in Scotland, including some in Edinburgh. Its website gives updated information about all the properties it is responsible for.

**www.historic-scotland.gov.uk**
The website has information on more than 300 listed buildings and ancient sites safeguarded by Historic Scotland.

## PRIME TRAVEL SITES

**www.fodors.com**
A complete travel-planning site. You can research prices and weather; reserve air tickets, cars and rooms; pose questions (and get answers) to fellow travellers; and find links to other sites.

**www.theAA.com**
Find out more about the wide range of travel publications and services the AA has to offer; click on hotels and B&B to find accommodation, or pubs and restaurants for eating and drinking options.

## CYBERCAFÉS

**Costa**
E8 ✉ 1 Hanover Street EH2 2DL ☎ 0131 226 4814 Mon–Sat 8am–8pm, Sun 10am–6pm £1 per 20 mins

**easyInternetcafé**
D8 ✉ 58 Rose Street EH2 2YQ ☎ 0131 220 3577 Daily 7.30am–10pm £1 per 30 mins

**Moviebank**
F7 ✉ 153 London Street EH3 6LX ☎ 0131 557 1011 Mon–Sat 11am–10pm, Sun noon–8pm 99p per 30 mins

# Getting There

## ENTRY REQUIREMENTS

Visitors from outside the UK must have a passport valid for at least six months from the date of entry. Citizens of EU member countries do not require a visa; US, Australian and Canadian visitors do not require a visa for stays of up to six months. Always check the latest information before you travel (www.ukvisas.gov.uk).

## MONEY

Scotland's currency is pounds sterling (£), in notes of £1, £2, £5, £10, £20, £50 and £100. Coins are issued in values of 1p, 2p, 5p, 10p, 20p, 50p, £1 and £2. England's notes are legal tender in Scotland.

£1

£5

£10

## ARRIVING

There are direct flights to Edinburgh's international airport from other parts of the UK and from continental Europe, but most transatlantic flights are routed via London. Airport facilities include an information desk, a few shops, bureaux de change, restaurants, car-rental firms and left-luggage.

13km (12 miles)
13km (8 miles)
6.5km (4 miles)

**Edinburgh International Airport**
Bus 20mins; £5 return

### FROM EDINBURGH INTERNATIONAL AIRPORT

Edinburgh's airport (☎ 0131 333 1000; www.baa.com) is located at Ingliston, 9.6km (6 miles) west of the city, off the A8.

Airlink operates a coach service to the heart of Edinburgh every 10 minutes on weekdays, less often at weekends and in the evening. The journey takes about 20 minutes and costs £5 return, £3 one-way. Tickets can be bought from Tourist Information inside the airport, from the ticket booth or on the bus. A map showing the route is available from the information desk and there is a map inside the bus. Buses leave from the arrivals area in front of the terminal building.

Taxis wait outside the arrivals hall in the rank beside the coach park. The journey takes about 25 minutes and costs around £15.

### ARRIVING BY RAIL

Edinburgh has two major rail stations: Edinburgh Haymarket and Edinburgh Waverley. Waverley is a main hub for onward travel within Scotland, and is well served with tourist information desks and other facilities. The main rail companies operating from England to

Edinburgh are Virgin and GNER and most internal services are run by Scotrail (☎ 0870 161 1061; **www.**scotrail.co.uk). For further details of fares and services contact the National Rail Enquiry Service (☎ 08457 484950; **www.**nationalrail.co.uk).

## Arriving by Coach

Coaches arrive in Edinburgh from England, Wales and all over Scotland at the St. Andrews Street bus station. The main coach companies operating to and from here are National Express (☎ 08705 808080; **www.**nationalexpress.com) and Scottish Citylink (☎ 08705 505050; **www.**citylink.co.uk).

## Getting Around

Lothian Buses (☎ 0131 555 6363; **www.** lothianbuses.co.uk) is the main bus company operating throughout the city (the buses are either maroon and white or red and white). Bus stops display the name of the stop and the bus numbers for regular and night services. Pay on boarding and ensure you have the exact fare as no change is given. Put the money into the slot in front of the driver, then take your ticket from the machine behind the driver. Standard adult fares for a single journey are 80p or £1; people eligible for a discount pay a 40p flat rate before 9.30am Mon–Fri, and travel free at all other times. A child aged 5–15 pays 50p to travel any distance. You can buy a Daysaver ticket from the driver for a day's unlimited travel (adult £2.50 and child £2 all day Mon–Fri, or £2 for an adult after 9.30 Mon–Fri and all day Sat and Sun).

Timetables and tickets are available at the Travel Shops (✉ 27 Hanover Street; Shandwick Place; Waverley Bridge ◉ Mon–Sat 8.30–6, Sun 9.30–5). An enlarged map and timetable on the bridge outside Waverley Station has additional information about the night bus service into the suburbs. Licensed taxis operate a reliable service day and night; fares are metered and strictly regulated. Cabs can be found at designated ranks like Waverley Park or Pollock, can be hailed along the road, or called by phone (City Cabs ☎ 0131 228 1211; Computer Cabs ☎ 0131 228 2555).

## DRIVING

One-way systems, narrow streets, 'red' routes and dedicated bus routes make driving in the city difficult. Limited on-street parking is mostly pay-and-display 8.30am–6.30pm Mon–Sat. There are designated parking areas, to the south of Princes Street; the biggest is at Greenside Place, off Leith Street.

## VISITORS WITH DISABILITIES

TRIPSCOPE (✉ The Vassall Centre, Gill Avenue, Bristol BS16 2QQ, ☎ Helpline 08457 585641; fax 0117 939 7736) offers a nationwide information service for people with mobility problems. Capability Scotland (✉ 11 Ellersly Road, Edinburgh EH12 6HY ☎ 0131 313 5510; **www.**capability-scotland.org.uk) can advise on travel requirements to ensure a less stressful trip.

A wide range of information for visitors with disabilities can be found in VisitScotland's publication *Practical Information for Visitors with Disabilities*, available from the tourist board or from tourist offices.

7

# Living
# Edinburgh

# Edinburgh Now

Above: *Crowds stroll in the Princes Street Gardens.*
Centre top: *Riding along the beach at Portabello.*
Centre bottom: *Exhibit at the Scottish National Gallery of Modern Art*

Edinburgh, the beautiful capital of Scotland, attracts many thousands of visitors every year. They come for many reasons; to seek their ancestral roots, to experience the Festival, to get a taste of what makes Scotland tick. Whatever the reason, few first-time visitors are prepared for the sheer beauty of the city and the richness of its history and culture. Edinburgh effortlessly combines its past with all that's best in 21st-century life, making it an increasingly popular, year-round destination and a jumping-off point for exploring the rest of Scotland.

## MORNINGSIDE AND A' THAT

• Edinburgh's two main, and most contrasting, districts are the Old Town, a medieval area sprawling around the castle, and the New Town, a serenely rational slice of 18th- to 19th-century grid-patterned real estate that's the city's most desirable address. Within these two you'll find the main sights, plenty of bars, accommodation, restaurants and some tempting shops. This central area is ringed with districts, such as Leith, once a separate port and now one of Edinburgh's most buzzing recreational areas. Those looking for quieter charms choose south-lying Bruntsfield, or the West End, the farther reaches of the New Town. Real money heads for the spacious villas and quiet streets of Murrayfield and above all, formerly genteel Morningside, now a classy and sophisticated neighbourhood.

Above: *The light and airy Princes Mall.*
Left: *Detail of the Edinburgh International Conference Centre*

Reminders of the past are everywhere in Edinburgh. The castle rises majestically over the tall tenements, narrow streets and dark *vennels* (alleyways) of the Old Town, while, to the north, the broad streets and spacious squares of the New Town are lined with gracious 18th-century buildings. Look closer, though, and it becomes clear that the city is no time warp, a tourist hub existing as a living museum or theme park of the Enlightenment. Scotland's official capital since 1532, Edinburgh today is home to the country's devolved government, whose parliament building, regardless of the final cost, is the public face of surging national confidence. Devolved regional government has created

## FACTS AND FIGURES

● Edinburgh is at a latitude of 55° 55′ N and a longitude of 3° 10′ W
● The city's highest point is Arthur's Seat at 251m (823ft)
● The population is around half a million
● The New Town is Europe's largest urban conservation area and contains more than 3,000 listed (landmark) buildings

11

Above: *Views of the city from the Midlothian Ski Centre.*
Centre: *Inside the National Gallery of Scotland*

### THE OLD TOWN FIRE

• On 7 December 2002, flames engulfed the Cowgate area of the Old Town, a World Heritage Site. Caused by an electrical fault, the fire was fanned by the air pockets and cramped buildings in the narrow streets, eventually causing damage that will cost an estimated £100 million to redevelop. Miraculously, no one was hurt.

hundreds of jobs and attracted PR firms, consultants, lobbyists, advisors and new businesses, while money has poured into new buildings associated with the city's enhanced status. The economy is dominated by the service sector, with the emphasis on financial services. Third only to London and Frankfurt on the European financial scene, Edinburgh is home to the global Royal Bank of Scotland and the Bank of Scotland. Their growth, and that of other modern Scottish businesses, has encouraged growing numbers of young, ambitious, highly paid professionals. It's these people, rather than the numerous visitors, who have truly fuelled the city's renaissance, turning the capital into a slick and stylish metropolis, whose quality of life is rated among the highest in the UK.

Burgeoning capital it may be, but Edinburgh still remains a small city. This is a place where the

commercial and political elite all know each other, with wheeling and dealing around the restaurant table still the order of the day on a scale unimaginable in larger European cities. For visitors, the spin-off is the manageable size of the city, with everything of interest lying within easy reach of the ever-increasing number of hotels.

Above: *Petit Paris is a popular Grassmarket restaurant on a sunny day*

## FESTIVAL TIME

• Edinburgh's Festival is not one event but many, running concurrently in August. The most prestigious is the Edinburgh International Festival, founded in 1947, which showcases world-class performing arts events. Side by side with this heavyweight, the anarchic and vast Fringe has theatre, music, comedy and dance in nearly 300 venues. The Edinburgh Jazz and Blues Festival is the UK's longest running jazz fest, and the Film Festival is up there with Cannes, Sundance and Venice. The International Book Festival is the largest in the world, while the Royal Military Tattoo holds its place as the most popular of all the events.

## PRINCES STREET

• Princes Street, despite its World Heritage status, has long been an architectural blot, a string of tasteless identikit buildings housing chain stores. Hope is at hand, with plans to demolish some of the worst buildings and replace them with quality shopping malls and expensive housing, a scheme due for completion by 2015.

13

Above: *A view up Victoria Street from Grassmarket.*
Above right: *Stopping for a coffee in Princes Street Gardens*

## TARTAN AT A PRICE

• Tartan has undergone a surge in popularity, but growth in desirability hasn't dented the price. The cost of a kilt is based on the amount of fabric and the workmanship involved in the manufacture and the detailing, with prices starting at around £120 for something basic and soaring to £600 for the best.

The transport system is more than adequate, walking is always an option and the authorities have poured money into revamping old, or building new, museums, galleries and attractions. The Festival and its famous Fringe has grown enormously, and the dark days of mid-winter are brightened by the huge celebrations at Hogmanay (New Year's Eve). Some locals may view the razzmatazz with mixed feelings, but the city in August undoubtably has an edge.

Not everyone benefits; Edinburgh still has pockets of dire poverty, and a drug problem that has seen the number of heroin addicts double over five years. The city's officials are striving to address this, and to tackle prejudice against immigration with a policy of cultural diversity.

For visitors, however, this remains firmly in the background. The public face of Edinburgh is friendly, the pace of life relaxed. Scots are outgoing, with time to chat and a genuine desire to please. There's as much pleasure to be had in wandering the streets and talking to the people as in rushing from the castle to the museums to

the shops. Take time to participate in pleasures enjoyed by local people—theatre, music, bar-hopping and the club scene—rather than a steady diet of tartan-obsessed Caledonian entertainment. Buy a picnic, and eat it in the beautiful gardens in Princes Street alongside the city's workers, with the castle making an unforgettable backdrop.

For still more space, remember that Edinburgh has superb countryside and coastline on its doorstep, and a choice of other towns and picturesque villages in every direction. Their castles and stately homes make great day trips and, at peak times, it's quite feasible to stay outside the city and come in for daily sightseeing.

To get a real handle on the city, it's worth considering a winter visit, when Edinburgh belongs firmly to its inhabitants, and the cold and wind add a new dimension. Whenever you visit, make it a pleasure, not a history lesson or a cultural marathon; in Edinburgh, there are sights and an atmosphere that will make your experience unique.

*Above left: Grassmarket has a strong café culture.*
*Above right: Crowds gather in Holyrood Park during the Festival*

### THE PRICE OF PARLIAMENT

● In the late 1990s, construction of a new parliament building was given the go-ahead at the price of £40 million. Costs rapidly escalated, and by 1999, £109 million was the target cost. When the new building finally opened in 2004, the projected final figure topped the £400 million mark.

# Edinburgh Then

Above: *The Mons Meg cannon at Edinburgh Castle.*
Above right: *James VI*

### EARLY SETTLERS

The area was first settled by hunting tribes around 3000BC and in about 1000BC the first farmers were joined by immigrant Beaker People, who introduced pottery and metalworking skills. Parts of Scotland were held by the Romans for a short time and after their departure in the 5th century AD the area suffered waves of invasion.

### THE MACALPINS

Northumbrians held southern Scotland for 33 years but were defeated in 1018 by MacAlpin king Malcolm II. Malcolm III married Margaret, sister of Edgar Atheling, heir to the English throne, but was usurped by William the Conqueror.

**1314** Thomas Randolph retakes Edinburgh Castle from the English on behalf of Robert the Bruce.

**1329** Edinburgh receives Royal Charter from Robert the Bruce.

**1349** Thirty per cent of Edinburgh's population is killed by the Black Death.

**1513** James IV is killed at the Battle of Flodden; work begins on Flodden Wall for the defence of Edinburgh.

**1544** Edinburgh is attacked by English forces, who fail to take the city.

**1566** Holyroodhouse is the scene of the Darnley's grizzly murder of David Rizzio, the favourite of Mary, Queen of Scots.

**1603** James VI moves his Court to London after acceding to the English throne.

**1633** Edinburgh officially becomes capital city of Scotland.

**1638** Signing of the National Covenant to defend the Scottish 'Kirk'.

**1639** Parliament House is built and used by the Scottish Parliament until 1707.

**1695** The Bank of Scotland is chartered.

**1692–8** A run of bad harvests leads to riots.

**1702–7** The Scottish Parliament debates and finally ratifies the Act of Union, voting itself out of existence.

**1736** The Porteous Riots.

**1767** First plans for New Town adopted.

**1817** *The Scotsman* is first printed.

**1824** The world's first municipal fire service is founded after fire rages for three days in the High Street.

**1890** Forth Rail Bridge opens.

**1895** Electric street lighting is introduced.

**1947** The first Edinburgh International Festival.

**1970** Commonwealth Pool and Meadowbank Stadium are built for the 1970 Commonweath Games.

**1971** St. James Centre opens and further demolition of Georgian houses in Princes Street takes place.

**1986** The Commonwealth Games is held in Edinburgh for a second time.

**1999** The Scottish Parliament sits for the first time since 1707.

**2004** The Queen opens the striking new Parliament building.

**2005** Trade Justice campaigners march through the city, before the G8 summit at Gleneagles.

Above: *An early etching of the city*

### EDINBURGH'S FAMOUS

Some of Edinburgh's most famous sons have had a significant impact on our lives. Alexander Graham Bell invented the telephone in 1847, and anaesthetics were pioneered by James Young Simpson. John Knox reformed Scotland's religion and architect Robert Adam and artists Henry Raeburn and Allan Ramsay brought their flair to the buildings of the city. The literary impact has been phenomenal through the romances of Sir Walter Scott, who was born in the city in 1771, and the detective stories of Sir Arthur Conan Doyle. More fame comes from Robert Louis Stevenson, author of *Kidnapped* and *Treasure Island,* who was born here in 1850, and actor Sean Connery, who spent his early days here.

# Time to Shop

*Below: The traditional elegance of Jenners*

Once overshadowed by the glitz of Glasgow, Edinburgh has now won serious shoppers from all over Scotland, as well as countless visitors. Shops in Princes Street may be little more than

## SHOPPING AREAS

The city's retail heart beats in Princes Street, and if you're looking for chain stores it's the best choice; if not, with the exception of the excellent department store Jenners, it can be avoided. For souvenirs, head for the Old Town, where tartan, tat, woollens and whisky crowd the shelves. The New Town's best shops are around Queen Street, with big-name, classy shopping at The Walk off St. Andrew's Square. For good local shops, head for Stockbridge, Bruntsfield and Morningside.

a string of high street names, and malls ring the suburbs, but away from these Edinburgh offers some of the best shopping in Europe. International names contrast with specialized outlets offering the best of Scottish products, and the goods and service of traditional retailers are hard to find elsewhere. These temples to commerce are housed in a wonderful variety of buildings, ranging through stolid Victorian respectability and glass-and-steel modernity to idiosyncratic one-man shops with a quirky charm all their own. The tip is to get off the main drags and into the side streets and alleyways to source everything from custom-made bagpipes to cashmere as soft as a cloud.

If you're looking for something typically Scottish, you'll be spoiled for choice whatever your budget. Woollens, tartans, tweeds and cashmeres are everywhere, and smaller stores sell one-off designer knitted goods in rainbow hues, or tartan with a twist, bringing Scottish style right into the 21st century. Local craftsmen are celebrated for their silver, metalwork and jewellery, and you'll find samples at the swanky city stores or among dozens of tiny studio-workshops. You can find the country's musical

Left: *Princes Street offers a good range of chain stores*

heritage in a huge range of CDs—everything from reels and pipe-and-drum music to Celtic Rock and traditional Gaelic song. Books, posters and calendars make great souvenirs and gifts, and you'll find an excellent selection in many book and gift shops. As a capital city, Edinburgh is also well endowed with expensive antiques shops and fine art and contemporary galleries, while other shops specialize in historic maps and antiquarian books with a Scottish theme. Urban sophisticates can bypass all this to home in on furniture and objets d'art that combine traditional craftsmanship with cutting-edge design, not just from Scotland but also from all over the world.

Food is always a popular souvenir, and shops sell the best of the country's produce, often vacuum-packed to make transportation easier. Take home wild smoked salmon, Orkney cheese, heather honey and soft fruit jam, shortbread, oatcakes and a bottle of finest malt whisky from the huge range you'll find.

## MARKETS

Sundays see thousands of locals heading out to Ingliston, which is home to a huge, cheap and vibrant outdoor market with more than 100 stalls and a car boot sale thrown in. Undercover markets include the rambling New Street Sunday Market in the Old Town. For the best in Scottish produce, the bi-monthly Saturday Farmers' Market, held on Castle Terrace, is worth a trawl for superb organic meat, vegetables and other foods.

19

# Out and About

*Below: Edinburgh Tour buses help you to explore the city. Below right: A carved column in Rosslyn Chapel*

## WALKING TOURS

**Mercat Walking Tours**
Walks where you can explore secret underground vaults, ghost walks and fascinating history tours with dramatic commentaries.
✉ Mercat House, Niddry Street South
☎ 0131 557 6464;
**www.**mercattours.com

**The Cadies and Witchery Tours**
Light-hearted ghostly tours through the darker parts of Old Edinburgh.
✉ 84 West Bow   ☎ 0131 225 6745; **www.**witchery tours.com

## INFORMATION

**NORTH BERWICK**
**Distance** 40km (25 miles)
**Travel time** 30 minutes
🚉 From Waverley
🛈 Quality Street
☎ 01620 892197
**Scottish Seabird Centre**
✉ The Harbour, North Berwick EH39 4SS
☎ 01620 890202;
www.seabird.org
🕐 Apr–end Oct daily 10–6; Nov–end Mar Mon–Fri 10–5, Sat, Sun 10–5.30 💷 Moderate

## ORGANIZED SIGHTSEEING

A guided tour is a good way to gain more in-depth knowledge about Edinburgh. If time is short, take one of the open-top buses that wind their way around the city sights; all tours depart from Waverley Bridge and there are four types to choose from, including one where you can hop on and hop off at your leisure (✉ 0131 220 0770; **www.**edinburghtour.com). Various companies offer coach tours in and around the city. Try Rabbie's Trail Burners (✉ 0131 226 3133) who run mini-coach (16 seater) tours to destinations such as Loch Ness and St. Andrews.

For those who prefer two wheels, another option is Adrian's Edinburgh City Cycle Tour (✉ 07966 447 206); a three-hour tour starting from Holyrood Palace gates with all equipment supplied. If you would rather rely on your own steam, walking tours to suit all interests are widely available (➤ panel). For more information check with the tourist office.

## EXCURSIONS
### NORTH BERWICK

Once a small fishing port, North Berwick has developed into a lively holiday resort. Pleasure craft crowd the little harbour and its splendid Victorian and Edwardian architecture suggests prosperity. The Scottish Seabird Centre uses the latest technology to take pictures of seabirds nesting on the nearby cliffs and islands, and there are interactive and multimedia displays to interest all the family. Behind the town is the cone of the North Berwick Law, a 187m (613ft) high volcanic plug, with fine views from the top.

## ROSSLYN CHAPEL

In a tiny mining village south of Edinburgh, this is the most mysterious building in Scotland, perched above Roslin Glen. Founded in 1446 by William St. Clair, Third Earl of Orkney, the church was to be a large cruciform structure, but only the choir was completed, along with sections of the east transept walls. It is linked with the Knights Templar and other secretive societies, and is even believed by some to be the hiding place of the Holy Grail. It has found increased fame through its connection with the best-selling novel *The Da Vinci Code* by Dan Brown. Inside is the finest example of medieval stone-carving in Scotland, if not Britain. Every part of roof rib, arch, corbel and pillar is encrusted with decorative work, including representations of Green Men, the Seven Deadly Sins and other religious themes. A highlight is the Apprentice Pillar, an orgy of winged serpents and spiralling strands of foliage. Still used as a place of worship, the chapel is also associated with Scott's poem *The Lay of the Last Minstrel*.

## SOUTH QUEENSFERRY

From 1129 until 1964, prior to the opening of the road suspension bridge, a ferry operated across the Firth of Forth from South Queensferry. The older, cantilevered rail bridge built in the late-19th century has become an icon of Scotland. Only a short ride outside Edinburgh, this little royal burgh is a great place to come and admire the two Forth bridges on a summer's evening.

To the west, Hopetoun House—which can only be reached easily by car—is a spectacular early 18th-century mansion built by William Bruce and William Adam. It is full of fine paintings, original furniture and other valuables. From the grounds there are more great views of the Forth bridges.

**INFORMATION**

**ROSSLYN CHAPEL**
**Distance** 11km (7 miles)
**Travel time** 20 minutes
✉ Roslin EH25 9PU
☎ 0131 440 2159;
www.rosslynchapel.org
🕐 Mon–Sat 10–5, Sun noon–4.45
🎟 Moderate
🚌 15A (Lothian bus); 62 (First bus)

**INFORMATION**

**SOUTH QUEENSFERRY**
**Distance** 16km (10 miles )
**Travel time** 20 minutes
🚆 From Waverley to Dalmeny station
🚌 X4, 43 (First Buses)
ℹ Forth Bridges Tourist Information Centre, by North Queensferry KY11 1HP ☎ 01383 417759
**Hopetoun House**
✉ South Queensferry EH30 9SL
☎ 0131 331 2451
🕐 Easter to mid-Sep daily 10–5.30 🎟 Expensive; grounds only moderate

# Walks

## INFORMATION

**Distance** 2km (1.25 miles)
**Time** 1 hour walking;
considerably more with
stops
**Start point** Canongate,
Royal Mile
➕ G8
**End point** High Street,
Royal Mile
➕ F8
🚌 35
🛈 Many in Grassmarket
and Victoria Street

Above: *Take time to browse
in the shops of Victoria
Street*

### SPIRES AND GABLES OF THE OLD TOWN

Start on the Royal Mile at Canongate, site of an old Augustian monastery and view the striking Dutch-style Canongate Kirk (➤ 52), built in 1688. Next door is The People's Story (➤ 44) and opposite Huntly House, housing the Museum of Edinburgh (➤ 54), both giving an excellent insight into the history of the city. Continue up the road, which becomes the High Street, and you will pass John Knox House (➤ 54, panel) on the right and the noisy Museum of Childhood on the left (➤ 42). At the next crossroads you can see the Tron Kirk, which currently houses the Old Town Information Centre (➤ 55). Continue down the High Street and you will see the forbidding St. Giles' Cathedral (➤ 38) on your left, with the Mercat Cross (➤ 53) outside.

Pass the cathedral and take the next left along Melbourne Place (George IV Bridge) and walk down to the Museum of Scotland (➤ 39). Cross the road to Greyfriars, at the end of which you will find Greyfriar's Kirk (➤ 36). Turn down Candlemaker's Row and keep bearing left until you come into Grassmarket (➤ 61)—you can divert here to the right into West Bow, which leads to Victoria Street for speciality shopping and a selection of good cafés. Returning to Grassmarket look for St. Andrew's Cross, railed and set into the cobbles, commemorating the gallows site. For a good view of the castle, at the bottom of Grassmarket in the left-hand corner take the Vennel, a series of steps up to the city wall.

Return to Grassmarket and cross to the far corner and take Granny's Green Steps up to the castle (➤ 31). Turn right and follow the castle along until you eventually come to the Hub, a redundant church with a high spire. Cross over into Lawnmarket to soak up the atmosphere of the Old Town and escape the crowds by wandering among some of the 200-year-old narrow wynds (closes). Continue along Lawnmarket and you are back in the High Street, the heart of the Royal Mile.

## GEORGIAN FAÇADES OF THE NEW TOWN

Start at the Scott Monument (➤ 35) in Princes Street. Walk as far as the national galleries, keeping the gardens on your left. Cross the road onto Hanover Street. Take the second turning on your left and walk along George Street. At the end is Charlotte Square, one of the finest examples of Georgian architecture in the city. Turn right and right again into Young Street. At the end, turn left and go down North Castle Street—novelist and poet Sir Walter Scott lived at No. 39—until you reach Queen Street. Cross the road and turn left and then take the next right down Wemyss Place. At the end go right onto Heriot Row, where you'll find the home of Robert Louis Stevenson.

When you reach Howe Street turn left and before the church in the middle of the street, turn left and walk along South East Circus Place. Admire the sweep of the Royal Circus as you bear right to join North East Circus Place. At the end turn right onto St. Vincent Street. Cross over into Great King Street and at the end turn right and then immediately left onto Drummond Place and continue ahead into London Street. At the roundabout turn right and walk up Broughton Street with its choice of good refreshment stops.

At the end of Broughton Street look to your left into Picardy Place, where you will see a statue of fictional detective Sherlock Holmes (➤ 57, panel). Turn right onto York Place, and then left into Elder Street. Take the next right down Multrees Walk, an up-and-coming pedestrianized designer shopping street. In front of you is St. Andrew Square, where you can't miss the lofty statue of Henry Dundas in the middle (➤ 57). Go round the square, turning left into North St. David Street. You will see the Scott Monument ahead guiding you back to Princes Street.

### INFORMATION

**Distance** 4km (2.5 miles)
**Time** 1 hour 30 minutes
**Start/end point** Scott Monument, Princes Street
▦ F8
🚌 3, 10, 17, 25, 44 and others
🍴 Olive Branch (➤ 69)

Above: *Robert Louis Stevenson, author of* Treasure Island *and* Dr Jeykyll and Mr Hyde, *lived at 17 Heriot Row*

# Edinburgh by Night

Above: *The Edinburgh Festival Theatre has the largest stage in Britain.*
Above right: *A view of the city from Calton Hill at twilight*

24

### HOGMANAY

Hogmanay is Scotland's New Year, and Edinburgh celebrates it in style with a four-day spectacle that includes concerts, street parties, live music, marching bands, processions and spectacular fireworks. The heart of the city is the focus, with some 100,000 tickets issued by ballot in October, but even outside the cordoned area there's plenty going on. You may find yourself participating in 'first footing', the tradition of visiting private houses armed with a lump of coal and a bottle of whisky to wish the inhabitants a 'Guid New Year'.

### MUSIC, THEATRE, DANCE AND FILM

Outside the Festival, Edinburgh has a year-round schedule of the performing arts, with theatre, music, opera, dance, ballet, comedy, folk music, rock and jazz all on offer, while cinemas show blockbusters and art house movies. You can find listings information in *The List* (**www.**list.co.uk), a fortnightly magazine that details every type of entertainment. It's also worth checking out **www.**theoracle.co.uk for the most up-to-date listings. Tickets for major performances can be booked through Ticketline (0870 748 9000; Mon–Sat 10–8, Sun 11–6) or at venues.

### CALMER PLEASURES

If you're looking for a quieter evening, the city looks fantastic after dark, with many landmark buildings illuminated. Take a stroll along Princes Street, or head for the Castle Esplanade or Calton Hill for sweeping views over the city. Except for the Festival weeks, restaurants in Edinburgh tend to wind down around 10pm, so don't expect to find much open later; eat around 8pm, then head for a stylish bar or traditional pub.

### DANCE THE NIGHT AWAY

Edinburgh's club scene is far more subdued than that of Glasgow, London or Manchester, and, as in many other cities, is often in a state of flux, with venues and clubs changing from one month to the next. Fridays and Saturdays are the big nights, when admission prices rise and places stay open later. You can track down likely spots in *The List* or the free Thursday sheet *Metro*, or pick up flyers in bars and music shops.

# EDINBURGH's
## top 25 sights

The sights are shown on the maps on the inside front cover and inside back cover, numbered **1**–**25** across the city

25

# Edinburgh Zoo

## HIGHLIGHTS

- 'Penguin Parade'
- Free Hilltop Safari rides
- Rare breeds
- Lion enclosure
- 'Magic Forest'
- Rainy weather trail
- Conservation trail
- Aerial walkway

## INFORMATION

**www.edinburghzoo.org.uk**

✚ Off map at A10; Locator map off A3

✉ Corstorphine Road EH12 6TS

☎ 0131 334 9171

🕐 Apr–end Sep daily 9–6; Oct, Mar daily 9–5; Nov–end Feb daily 9–4.30

🍴 Restaurant, café, kiosks and picnic areas

🚌 12, 26, 31

♿ Very good

💰 Expensive

**Long gone are the days of the solitary sad elephant—this fine zoo provides the visitor with an inspirational day out while promoting the conservation of threatened species and habitats.**

**Conservation, education and fun** Located at Corstorphine, 5km (3 miles) west of the city centre, Edinburgh Zoo is on the side of a steep hill, covering an area of some 33ha (82 acres). In an era when zoos have to work hard to justify themselves, Edinburgh remains an excellent example of its type, allowing close access to around 1,000 animals. It successfully promotes conservation and education, while demonstrating how a visitor attraction can adapt to survive.

**Natural habitats** The new generation of animal exhibits have brought the crowds back—examples include the aerial walkway across the rolling hillocks occupied by the painted hunting dogs, and the African plains. Several other artfully designed enclosures give a sense of spaciousness, including the lion enclosure and the Magic Forest, with its small rainforest monkeys.

**Penguin parades** The zoo is particularly associated with penguins, with a history of successful breeding. The underwater views of the birds swimming are fascinating. Don't miss the daily stroll outside their enclosure by the penguins at 2.15, from April to September, weather permitting. Overall, a visit to the zoo, both for the animals and for the city views, should still be very much a part of the Edinburgh experience.

# Scottish National Gallery of Modern Art

**The gallery opened at this parkland site in 1984, providing an ideal setting for the work of those in the forefront of modern art: Matisse, Picasso, Hirst, you'll find them all here.**

**Setting the scene** The first thing you see as you arrive at the main gallery is a sweeping, living sculpture of grassy terraces and semicircular ponds, an installation called *Landform UEDA* by Charles Jencks. After such a grand introduction the rest of the gallery seems quite small, but it is certainly large in terms of its enviable and varied collection of modern art from around the world. It is housed in a former school.

**On display** Regularly changing exhibitions occupy the ground floor, with a varied display from the gallery's collection on the first floor. Among these pieces, look out for works by Picasso, Braque and Matisse, Hepworth and Gabo. The work of the early 20th-century group of painters known as the Scottish Colourists is particularly striking, with canvases by Samuel John Peploe (1871–1935), George Leslie Hunter (1877–1931), John Duncan Fergusson (1874–1961) and Francis Cadell (1883–1937). Also of interest are Fergusson's dramatic *Portrait of a Lady in Black* (c.1921), the vibrant colours of Cadell's *Blue Fan* (c.1922) and Peploe's later, more fragmentary work such as *Iona Landscape, Rocks* (c.1927).

**More modern art** Stroll across the road to the Dean Gallery (▶ 56), an outstation of the Gallery of Modern Art, where you can see various works by Dada and the Surrealists. If you're on the free gallery bus, visit the main gallery first and return to the town from the Dean Gallery.

## HIGHLIGHTS

- Works by the Scottish Colourists, including those by John Duncan Fergusson
- Major works by Picasso, Matisse and Lichtenstein
- Sculptures by Henry Moore and Barbara Hepworth
- Works by contemporary artists including Damien Hirst and Rachel Whitehead

## INFORMATION

www.nationalgalleries.org
- B8; Locator map off A3
- 75 Belford Road EH4 3DR
- 0131 624 6200
- Fri–Wed 10–5, Thu 10–7
- Gallery Café
- 13; free bus links all five national galleries
- Edinburgh Haymarket
- Very good
- Free, but may be charges for temporary exhibitions
- Shop stocks books, cards, gifts

# Royal Botanic Garden

**Known locally as The Botanics, these gardens boast some 15,500 species, one of the largest collections of living plants in the world. Possibly Edinburgh's finest recreational asset.**

**City greenery** Occupying this site since 1823, the gardens cover over 28ha (69 acres) of beautifully landscaped and wooded grounds to the north of the city, forming an immaculately maintained green oasis. The garden is walkable from Princes Street via Stockbridge, though you may wish to take the bus back up the hill. It is especially suitable for children as it is dog-free, although the squirrels can be persistent.

**Inside or out?** There are ten greenhouses to explore, collectively called the Glasshouse Experience and offering a perfect haven on cold days. They include an amazingly tall palm house dating back to 1858, and the Tropical Aquatic House, with its giant waterlilies and an underwater view of fish swimming through the lilies' roots. Outside, the plants of the Chinese Hillside and the Heath Garden are particularly interesting, and in summer the herbaceous borders are breathtaking. Check out the rhododendron collection and the rock garden, which displays some 5,000 species and is best seen in May. The highest point of the garden has a fine view of the city.

**Striking design** The West Gate, or Carriage Gate, is the main entrance, but don't miss the stunning inner east side gates, designed by local architect Ben Tindall in 1996. A riot of electroplated steel, they depict rhododendron foliage. Finally, take a look at the exhibitions of contemporary art and photography that are held in buildings around the site.

## HIGHLIGHTS

- Rock Garden
- Glasshouse Experience
- Tropical Aquatic House
- Chinese Hillside
- Scottish Heath Garden
- The gates

## INFORMATION

www.rbge.org.uk

✛ D5; Locator map A1

✉ 20A Inverleith Row
   EH3 5LR

☎ 0131 552 7171

🕒 Apr–end Sep daily 10–7;
   Mar, Oct daily 10–6;
   Nov–end Mar daily 10–4

🍴 Terrace Café

🚌 8, 17, 23, 27, also on
   Guide Friday and
   Mactours routes

🚉 Edinburgh Waverley

♿ Good

💷 Moderate charge for the
   glasshouses; tours
   moderate

❓ Tours lasting around 90
   minutes leave the West
   Gate at 11 and 2,
   Apr–end Sep. Extensive
   Botanics gift shop with
   stationery, plants and
   related souvenirs

# Georgian House

**This elegant house, with its preserved period interiors, gives you the chance to glimpse into the lives of the prosperous classes who lived in the New Town in the 18th century.**

**How the other half lived** The north side of Charlotte Square is the epitome of 18th-century New Town elegance and was designed by architect Robert Adam (1728–92) as a single, palace-fronted block. With its symmetrical stonework, rusticated base and ornamented upper levels, it is an outstanding example of the style. The Georgian House, a preserved residence on the north side of the square, oozes gracious living. It is a meticulous re-creation by the National Trust for Scotland, reflecting all the fashionable details of the day, right down to the Wedgwood dinner service on the dining table and the magnificent drawing room with its candlesticks aglitter. Exquisite paintings and graceful furniture complete the picture. This place was for the affluent, those who could afford to escape the cramped conditions of Edinburgh's Old Town and move to the elegant New Town.

**Georgian elegance** The 18th-century monied classes knew what they wanted. As you step in the door of this house you can't help but be impressed by the balustraded staircase and its stunning cupola above, flooding the building with light. The stairs lead to the first floor and the Grand Drawing Room, perfect for entertaining guests and giving recitals.

**Below stairs** For a contrast, take a look in the basement at the kitchen and the well-scrubbed areas, including the wine cellar and china closet. Here the hard work took place, reflecting the marked social divides of the time.

## HIGHLIGHTS

- Staircase and cupola
- Grand Drawing Room
- Dining Room
- Basement with kitchen

## INFORMATION

- www.nts.org.uk
- D8; Locator map A2
- 7 Charlotte Square EH2 4DR
- 0131 226 3318
- Apr–end Oct daily 10–5; Mar, Nov–end Dec daily 11–3
- 13, 19, 36, 37, 41
- Edinburgh Waverley
- Limited; six steps to ground floor
- Moderate
- New Town (➤ 32)

*Wedgwood and silver in the Dining Room*

29

# Princes Street and Princes Street Gardens

### HIGHLIGHTS

- Great views to the castle
- Jenner's department store (the world's oldest)
- Floral clock
- Summer band concerts

### INFORMATION

- D9–F8; Locator map A3–B3
- Princes Street
- Gardens: 7am–10pm summer, 7–5 winter
- Edinburgh Waverley
- Free
- New Town (➤ 32), Scott Monument (➤ 35)

**Originally designed as a residential area, the most famous street in Scotland is now where local people come to shop. The gardens are a welcome escape from the urban buzz.**

**Changes over time** If you stroll along Queen Street today, you can see how it echoes Princes Street and gives an insight to Craig's original residential plan. He designated today's Thistle and Rose streets, lesser byways between the grand thoroughfares, as the living and business place of tradesmen and shopkeepers. The use of the lanes behind Thistle and Rose streets to reach the back doors of the wealthier residents was a clever element in his deceptively simple scheme. Princes Street did not remain residential for long. The main tide of commercial developments began to flow from east to west by the mid-19th century. The gracious Georgian buildings began to deteriorate, some replaced by grim, practical edifices in the 20th century.

*The gardens were laid out for the public in 1820*

**Getting its name** Princes Street was originally to be called St. Giles Street, but King George III objected as it reminded him of the St. Giles district of London, which was notorious for its lowlife. So the most famous street in Scotland became Prince's Street after the Prince Regent, assuming its plural form in 1848.

**Oasis of green** Princes Street Gardens are a pleasant place to sit down and admire the backs of the Old Town tenements across the valley. In summer there are band concerts to enjoy, and an Edinburgh institution since 1902, the floral clock—a flowerbed planted up as a clock, complete with moving hands—can be found at the Waverley Station end.

# Edinburgh Castle

**Perched high on a wedge of volcanic rock, the castle is a symbol of the Scottish nation, reflecting 1,000 years of history. With its rich mix of architectural styles it should not be missed.**

**Might and majesty** As you wind your way up the Castle Rock you can enjoy the spectacular view north over the city. The cannons along the battery were a picturesque improvement suggested by Queen Victoria. The One o' Clock Gun, a 25-pounder field gun from World War II, fires from Mills Mount Battery at precisely 1pm in a tradition dating from 1861. To enter the castle you must first cross the Esplanade, the setting for the annual Military Tattoo (➤ 62).

**Once inside** The oldest structure in the castle is the 12th-century chapel, dedicated to St. Margaret by her son, King David I. The chapel is almost overshadowed by the huge cannon on the rampart outside—Mons Meg, a gift in 1457 to James II from the Duke of Burgundy.

**Castle of contrasts** One of the newest buildings on Castle Rock is the strikingly austere National War Memorial (➤ 52). Be prepared for crowds in The Crown Room where both the Scottish Crown Jewels and The Stone of Destiny are displayed. The crown dates from 1540 and is made of Scottish gold, studded with semi-precious stones from the Cairngorms. The sword and sceptre were both papal gifts. The Stone of Destiny was the stone on which Scottish kings were crowned—pinched by Edward I, it was recovered from Westminster Abbey in 1996. Down in the vaults is the castle's newest exhibition 'Prisoners at War'. The castle also contains the National War Museum of Scotland (➤ 55).

## HIGHLIGHTS

- Great views from the Castle Rock
- St. Margaret's Chapel
- Mons Meg
- Vaults
- Scottish Crown Jewels
- Stone of Destiny
- Scottish War Memorial
- One o' Clock Gun

## INFORMATION

www.historic-scotland.gov.uk
- E9; Locator map B3
- Castlehill EH1 2NG
- 0131 225 9846
- Apr–end Oct daily 9.30–6; Nov–end Mar daily 9.30–5
- Cafés
- 23, 27, 35, 41, 42
- Edinburgh Waverley
- Some areas are restricted, telephone first. A courtesy minibus is available to take less mobile people to the top of the castle site—check when you buy your ticket
- Expensive
- Royal Mile (➤ 37)
- The Esplanade in front of the castle doubles as a pay-and-display car park Nov–end May. Free guided tours every half-hour from just inside the main gate; hand-held audio guide in six languages. Gift shops stocking books, Scottish souvenirs and exclusive jewellery

31

# New Town

## INFORMATION

✚ C7–F8; Locator map
   A2–C2
ℹ Edinburgh Lothian Tourist
   Information Centre, 3
   Princes Street EH2 2QP
   ☎ 0131 473 3800
🚉 Edinburgh Waverley

**A product of the lack of space in Edinburgh's Old Town, this spectacular piece of Georgian town planning was instigated by a competition in 1766 to build a fine 'New Town'.**

**Georgian streets** Edinburgh's so-called New Town covers an area of about 318ha (1sq mile) to the north of Princes Street, and is characterized by broad streets of spacious terraced houses with large windows and ornamental door arches. The original area comprised three residential boulevards to run parallel with the Old Town ridge: Princes Street, George Street and Queen Street. With a square at each end (St. Andrew and Charlotte), they were also linked by smaller roads to take shops and other commercial services: Rose Street and Thistle Street. While Princes Street has lost its shine through commercial activity, wide Charlotte Square, with its preserved Georgian House (▶ 29), is the epitome of the planners' intentions.

**Other highlights** It took 2 million cartloads of rubble to create The Mound, later home to the National Gallery (▶ 34) and the Royal Academy Building. The Mound came about by accident, when 'Geordie' Boyd, a clothier in the Old Town, started to dump earth rubble in the marsh. Soon the builders from the New Town joined in as they dug out foundations for the new buildings. Another highlight of New Town is Stockbridge, a former mining village developed as part of the second New Town. It was on land owned by the painter Sir Henry Raeburn and went on to become a Bohemian artisans' corner. Ann Street is now one of the city's most exclusive addresses.

*Above: Moray Place is typical of the New Town.*
*Top: The slopes of The Mound*

# Scotch Whisky Heritage Centre

**Whisky is synonymous with Scotland and here you can learn about its 300-year history. Interactive displays let you experience related sights, sounds and smells, and you can finish with a taste!**

**Whisky galore** This popular attraction is located at the top of the Royal Mile immediately below the castle. Learn everything there is to know about Scotland's national tipple on a tour that sets off every 15 minutes and lasts around an hour. The voyage of discovery takes in a short film, a slow-moving barrel ride through history, and a talk through the manufacturing process. With models and a 'ghost'—a Master Blender from 150 years ago—it's a better all-round family fun experience than most distillery tours, which can be very technical. Adults get a free taste (juice for children), and you can then, if you are up to it, explore more than 270 whiskies and liqueurs at the Whisky Barrel Bar.

**On the whisky trail** The problem with whisky-making is that it is not a dramatic process. It takes patience and time. Fortunately the Scotch Whisky Heritage Centre injects fun into the subject with its high-tech talking tableaux and commentary, all viewed while riding along on a hollowed-out whisky barrel. En route you will come face to face with the characters who shaped the Scotch whisky industry. Delve into the intricate secrets of whisky making, including 'nosing'—how smell can influence the way you perceive taste—and blending. And you can see the whole process through the fascinating mechanical model built to represent Tormore Distillery, found beside the River Spey. If all this doesn't whet your appetite to sample a wee dram, then it is doubtful anything ever will!

## HIGHLIGHTS

- Barrel ride
- Meet the whisky ghost
- Mechanical distillery model
- Tasting a dram

## INFORMATION

www.whisky-heritage.co.uk

- E9; Locator map B3
- 354 Castlehill, The Royal Mile EH1 2NE
- 0131 220 0441
- May–end Sep daily 9.30–6.30; Oct–end Apr daily 10–6
- Amber Restaurant
- 23, 27, 35, 41, 42
- Edinburgh Waverley
- Very good
- Expensive
- Royal Mile (➤ 37)

Above: *Visitors on the barrel ride through the Scotch Whisky Heritage Centre*

# National Gallery of Scotland

## INFORMATION

**www.**nationalgalleries.org

⊞ E9; Locator map B3

✉ The Mound EH2 2EL

☎ 0131 624 6200

🕐 Daily 10–5, Thu until 10pm

🍴 Café

🚌 3, 10, 17, 23, 24, 27, 44 and others; free bus links all five national galleries

🚉 Edinburgh Waverley

♿ Very good

🎟 Free

↔ Princes Street and Gardens (►30), New Town (►32)

🛍 Shop stocks cards, books and gifts

**This striking mid-19th-century Classical revival building houses superb Old Masters and an outstanding Scottish collection. It is the perfect setting for Scotland's finest art.**

**Artistic venue** The gallery was designed by New Town architect William Playfair (1789–1857) and completed in the year of his death. It is easily spotted from the huge golden stone pillars of its neoclassical flanks and should not be confused with its neighbour, the Royal Scottish Academy, which has been refurbished as an international exhibition venue (►56).

**What's on show** The gallery's collection of paintings, sculptures and drawings runs to more than 20,000 items, displayed in intimate and accessible surroundings. At its heart are paintings by the great masters of Europe, including Vermeer, Hals, Tiepolo, Van Dyck, Raphael and Titian. Look out for Monet's *Haystacks* (1891), Vélasquez's *Old Woman Cooking Eggs* (1618) and Botticelli's masterpiece *Virgin Adoring the Sleeping Christ Child* (c.1485). A fabulous collection of watercolours by English landscape artist J.M.W. Turner (1775–1851) is displayed in January each year.

**Scottish contingent** Not surprisingly, the gallery has an outstanding collection of works by Scottish artists. Favourites here include the unusual 1795 portrait of *The Reverend Robert Walker Skating*, and the sweeping land- and seascapes of William McTaggart (1835–1910). Look out for the vivid scenes of everyday life among the common people, as captured on canvas by Sir David Wilkie (1785–1841), such as *Pitlessie Fair* (1804) and *Distraining for Rent* (1815).

*The new Weston link*

## Scott Monument

**Generations have climbed this 61m (200ft) structure since it opened in 1846 to appreciate fine views of the city. Take a closer look at the stone figures, characters from Scott's novels.**

**Make the effort** It is well worth the draughty climb up the 287 steps to the top of this Gothic sandstone pinnacle that dominates the eastern end of Princes Street. You'll be rewarded with wonderful views to the castle.

**Scotland's literary hero** When Sir Walter Scott died in 1832, Edinburgh's officials decided a fitting monument should be built to this most outstanding of writers. An architectural competition was launched in 1836 to find the most appropriate memorial. It was finally built, after permission was granted by Parliament to build in Princes Street Gardens, between 1840 and 1846, to the design of George Meikle Kemp, a grandiose riot of ornate Gothicism. It was later encrusted with stone based on characters from Scott's novels. A statue of the novelist, with his favourite deerhound Maida, sits at the bottom. In contrast to the sandstone of the building, the statue is in Italian Carrara marble. It is by John Steel (1804–91), who also carved the figure of Prince Albert on London's Albert Memorial.

**Opt out** If you start to falter on your long climb up you can always pause for breath at the first floor level. Here there is a small room with displays about Scott's life and work. You can also use the headphones to listen to readings and musical settings of his novels.

### HIGHLIGHTS

- Views over the city
- Stone figures of Sir Walter Scott's characters
- Statue of Scott at the base

### INFORMATION

www.cac.org.uk
- F8; Locator map C3
- East Princes Street Gardens EH2 2EJ
- 0131 529 4068
- Apr–end Sep Mon–Sat 9–6, Sun 10–6; Oct–end Mar Mon–Sat 9–3, Sun 10–3
- Edinburgh Waverley
- Inexpensive
- Princes Street and Gardens (▶ 30), New Town (▶ 32), National Gallery of Scotland (▶ 34)

*An autumnal view of the monument*

# Greyfriars Kirk

- Greyfriars Bobby
- Elaborate 17th-century memorials
- Peaceful surroundings

## INFORMATION

www.greyfriarskirk.com

✠ F9; Locator map C3

✉ Greyfriars Tolbooth and Highland Kirk, Greyfriars Place EH1 2QQ

☎ 0131 226 5429

🕐 Apr–end Oct Mon–Fri 10.30–4.30, Sat 10.30–2.30; Nov–end Mar Thu 1.30–3.30

🚌 27, 35, 41, 42

🚉 Edinburgh Waverley

♿ Very good

🎫 Free

↔ Museum of Scotland (► 39)

*Edinburgh's most famous canine hero*

**Built in 1620 on the site of the garden of a former Franciscan monastery, the Kirk of the Grey Friars has had a turbulent history. Today it is a peaceful haven for quiet contemplation.**

**Battleground** Just 18 years after the church was built, it was the scene of a pivotal event in Scottish history, when Calvinist petitioners gathered to sign the National Covenant, an act of defiance against the king, Charles I. The church itself was trashed by Cromwell's troops in 1650, and later accidentally blown up. In the kirkyard a makeshift prison was erected to house hundreds of Covenanters captured after the battle of Bothwell Bridge in 1679; they were kept here for five dreadful months. Today it is full of elaborate memorials, including the grave of architect William Adam (1689–1748).

**Undying loyalty** Opposite the churchyard gate stands a popular Edinburgh landmark: a fountain with a bronze statue of a little Skye terrier, which has stood here since 1873. The dog's story was told by American Eleanor Atkinson in her 1912 novel *Greyfriars Bobby*. He was the devoted companion of a local farmer who dined regularly in Greyfriars Place. After his master died, faithful Bobby slept on his grave in the nearby churchyard for 14 years. A later version suggests he was owned by a local policeman, and taken in by local residents when his owner died. There is a portrait of Bobby, painted by John MacLeod in 1867, inside the church.

**Scottish worship** Greyfriars welcomes visitors to all its services, in particular the regular Gaelic service held at 12.30 on Sundays. It is the only regular weekly Gaelic worship conducted in southeastern Scotland.

## Royal Mile

**Stretching downhill from Edinburgh Castle to Holyrood Palace, the Royal Mile is a focal point for visitors who like to explore the narrow wynds leading off the main thoroughfare.**

**Origins of the mile** The Royal Mile is the long, almost straight street leading up the spine of rock on which the Old Town was built. Lined with medieval tenement houses, this part of the city became so overcrowded that a New Town (► 32) had to be built in the 18th century. About 60 narrow closes or wynds lead off between the buildings on either side, with names, such as Fleshmarket, indicating the trades once carried out there.

**Down to earth** The new Scottish Parliament Building (► 45) dominates the Holyrood end of the Royal Mile. From here, the area around Canongate is practical and workaday, the dressed stone of its façades giving way to rough stonework on the sides of the buildings. You can see a view of the interiors of these old houses at the Museum of Edinburgh (► 54). Look for a board outside the Canongate Church, indicating the famous buried there.

**Onwards and upwards** At the crossing of St. Mary's Street and Jeffrey Street you enter the High Street. Above the Tron Kirk the road retains its setts (cobbles) and broadens out. After St. Giles' Cathedral, with the Heart of Midlothian in the cobbles marking the site of a prison, the street becomes the Lawnmarket, with its fine 16th- and 17th-century tenements, where linen (lawn) was manufactured. The final stretch lies above The Hub (a converted church), as the road narrows on the steep approach to the castle.

### HIGHLIGHTS

- Narrow closes, wynds and vennels (alleys)
- Tenement houses
- Canongate Church

### INFORMATION

- ✚ E9–H8; Locator map B3–E3
- ✉ The Royal Mile
- 🚌 23, 35, 41 and others
- ↔ Edinburgh Castle (► 31), Scotch Whisky Heritage Centre (► 33), St. Giles' Cathedral (► 38), Palace of Holyrood House (► 48)

*More than 300 whiskies are available at Royal Mile Whiskies*

## St. Giles' Cathedral

### INFORMATION

**www.stgiles.net**
- F9; Locator map C3
- High Street EH1 1RE
- 0131 225 9442
- May–end Sep Mon–Fri 9–7, Sat 9–5, Sun 1–5; Oct–end Apr Mon–Sat 9–5, Sun 1–5 (and for services year round)
- Cathedral Restaurant
- 23, 27, 35, 41
- Edinburgh Waverley
- Very good
- Free
- Royal Mile (▶ 37)

**Imposing, and its dark stonework somewhat forbidding, the High Kirk of Edinburgh stands near the top of the Royal Mile. It is dedicated to St. Giles, the patron saint of the city.**

**Origins of the building** The columns inside the cathedral that support the 49m (160ft) tower, with its distinctive crown top, are a relic of the 12th-century church that once occupied this site. The tower itself dates from 1495, and the rest of the church from the 15th and 16th centuries. This tower, whose crown was completed in 1500, is one of the few remaining examples of 15th-century work to be seen in the High Street today. Much of the church has been altered and reworked over subsequent centuries.

**Saintly beginnings** St. Giles' parish church—it became a cathedral in the mid-17th century—was probably founded by Benedictine followers of Giles. He was a 7th-century hermit (and later abbot and saint) who lived in France, a country with strong ties with Scotland. In 1466, the Preston Aisle of the church was completed, in memory of William Preston who had acquired the arm bone of the saint in France. This relic disappeared in about 1577, but St. Giles' other arm bone is still in St. Giles' Church, Bruges.

**Famous sons** Presbyterian reformer John Knox (c.1513–72) became minister here in 1559, arguing openly against Mary, Queen of Scots' attempts to revive the Roman Catholic cause. The body of the great soldier James Graham, Marquis of Montrose (1612–50), is interred here, and there is a bronze memorial to writer Robert Louis Stevenson (1850–94), who died in Samoa. Inside, the exquisitely carved Thistle Chapel is by architect Robert Lorimer (1864–1929).

*Detail of a stained-glass window*

# Museum of Scotland

**An unashamedly modern castle protecting Scotland's national treasures. Designed by Benson & Forsyth, it incorporates the original 18th-century museum and was opened in 1998.**

**So much to see** Treasures abound in this superb collection, but it can be confusing to find your way around and you won't see it all in one visit. Work your way up chronologically from the basement through history from the earliest beginnings. Check out the section on early people, with its fascinating sculptures by Eduardo Paolozzi decked out in ancient jewellery. The museum's floors follow the history of Scotland, through its Gaelic heritage, the impact of Christianity and the Union with England in 1707. Subsequent galleries display associations with culture, industry and emigration, and the impact of the Scottish nation on the world.

**Pick of the highlights** Well worth a look are the displays of the Pictish period: vivid relief carvings in stone. Don't miss the Hunterston brooch dating from around AD700, a potent symbol of wealth and power. No contemporary clasp in the museum's collection can touch it in terms of size (about 12cm/5ins high) or craftsmanship. Although the lighting is dim, you can see the detail of the gold, amber and gilded silver worked into curling, intertwined Celtic motifs. Another highlight is the collection of 82 carved chess pieces discovered in the sands of Uig, on Lewis in 1831; these small 12th-century greyish figures are carved from walrus ivory. And for an unusual slant on Scotland's national bard, take at look at Burns' pistols.

## HIGHLIGHTS

- Pictish carvings (level 0)
- Hunterston brooch (level 0)
- Lewis chess pieces (level 1)
- Burns' pistols (level 3)
- Eduardo Paolozzi sculptures (level 0)
- Great views from roof

## INFORMATION

www.nms.ac.uk
- F9; Locator map C3
- Chambers Street EH1 1JF
- 0131 247 4422
- Mon–Sat 10–5 (Tue until 8pm), Sun 12–5
- Tower Restaurant (► 65); reservations essential at weekends. Various cafés available in the Royal Museum
- 3, 3A, 7, 8, 14, 23, 27, 29, 31, 33, 41, 42
- Very good
- Free; charge for some temporary exhibitions
- Gift shop, shared with the Royal Museum, stocks unusual presents. Check on the information desk on arrival for times of free daily tours. Free audio guides available in English, Gaelic, French and German
- Greyfriars Kirk (► 36)

*Music is an important part of Scotland's heritage*

# Royal Yacht *Britannia*

## HIGHLIGHTS

- Royal Apartments
- Drawing Room
- State Dining Room
- Sun Lounge
- Royal Bedrooms
- Sick Bay & Operating Theatre
- Engine Room
- The Bridge

## INFORMATION

www.royalyachtbritannia.co.uk
- H2; Locator map off E1
- 309 off E1, Ocean Terminal, Leith EH6 6JJ
- 0131 555 5566
- Mar–end Oct daily 9.30–6 (last admission 4.30); Nov–end Feb daily 10–5 (last admission 3.30)
- Café in visitor centre
- 1, 11, 22, 34, 35, 36
- Edinburgh Waverley
- Excellent
- Expensive
- Leith (► 41)
- Reservations strongly advised in high season

**This former royal yacht is one of the world's most famous ships, now moored in Edinburgh's historic port of Leith. It is 83rd in a long line of royal yachts stretching back to 1660.**

**New role** *Britannia* was decommissioned in 1997 after a cut in government funds. It had carried the Queen and her family on 968 official voyages all over the world since its launch at Clydebank in 1953. Now it's a floating museum at Edinburgh's port of Leith, accessed via the Ocean Terminal shopping and leisure complex.

**Vital statistics** For 40 years, *Britannia* served the royal family, travelling over one million miles to become the most famous ship in the world. A compact yacht, it is just 125.6m (412ft) long. She carried a crew of 240, including a Royal Marine band and an additional 45 household staff when the royal family were aboard. The on-shore visitor centre sets the scene, telling the history of the ship. A self-guided tour using handsets takes you around the yacht itself. *Britannia* still retains the fittings and furnishings of her working days, which gives an intimate insight into the royals away from usual palace protocol.

**Royal and naval precision** Check out the apartments adorned with hundreds of original items from the royal collection. The grandest room is the State Dining Room, and the most elegant the Drawing Room. Imagine the royal family relaxing in the Sun Lounge; view the modest sleeping quarters, including the bedroom where Prince Charles and other members of the family honeymooned. Everything on board is ship-shape, from the Engine Room and the Bridge to the fully equipped Sick Bay and Laundry.

## Leith

**Edinburgh's seaport, amalgamated with the city in 1921, has been a dock area since the 14th century. Following a decline in shipbuilding, it has been regenerated into a trendy tourist area.**

**New role** Leith was for many years a prosperous town in its own right. As the shipbuilding industry began to wane in the 20th century the town went into decline, but in recent years it has come up in the world, and now it buzzes with fashionable eating places. The area known as the Shore, along the waterfront, has been well restored and is filled with flourishing bars and restaurants. Warehouses, once full of wine and whisky, have been converted into smart accommodation. Where Tower Street meets The Shore, look for the Signal Tower, built in 1686 as a windmill. Edinburgh's river, the Water of Leith, flows through the middle of the town and you can visit the visitor centre to learn more about its wildlife and heritage.

**Historic Leith** The town has witnessed its share of history—Mary, Queen of Scots, landed here from France in 1561 and stayed at Lamb House, in Water Street. One of the earliest references made to golf was when James II of Scotland banned the sport from Leith links as it interfered with the army's archery practice. Charles I played golf on the links in the park. The original 13 rules of golf were drawn up here in 1744 but in 1907 the dunes were levelled to create a public park and golf was banned once more.

**Modern development** For visitors, the Royal Yacht *Britannia* is the draw, and to access the ship you enter through the 2001 complex, the Ocean Terminal, one of Europe's largest shopping and leisure complexes, including a 12-screen cinema.

### HIGHLIGHTS

- The Shore
- Bars and restaurants
- Water of Leith Visitor Centre
- Royal Yacht *Britannia*

### INFORMATION

- ✠ G1–K4; Locator map off E1
- ✉ Leith
- 🚌 1, 11, 16, 22, 34, 35, 36
- ↔ Royal Yacht *Britannia* (▶ 40)
- ℹ For information: Edinburgh Lothian Tourist Information Centre, 3 Princes Street EH2 2QP
  ☎ 0131 473 3800

# Museum of Childhood

**This has been described as 'the noisiest museum in the world' and it is popular with both children and adults. Introduce your children to the past and maybe relive it yourself.**

## HIGHLIGHTS

- Extensive toy collection
- Re-creation of 1930s classroom
- Victorian dolls
- Dolls' houses
- Automata

## INFORMATION

www.cac.org.uk
- ✚ G9; Locator map D3
- ✉ 42 High Street, Royal Mile EH1 1TG
- ☎ 0131 529 4142
- 🕐 Mon–Sat 10–5; also Jul–Aug Sun noon–5
- 🚌 35 and all North Bridge buses
- 🚉 Edinburgh Waverley
- ♿ Very good
- 🎫 Free
- ↔ Royal Mile (➤ 37)

**Nostalgic pleasure** The Museum of Childhood is a delight and claims to be the first museum in the world dedicated to the history of childhood. It was the brainchild of town councillor Joseph Patrick Murray, who argued that the museum was about children rather than for them. Opened in 1955, the collection has grown to display a nostalgic treasure trove of dolls and dolls' houses, train sets and teddy bears. Every aspect of childhood is covered here, from education and medicine to clothing and food. Don't miss the re-created 1930s schoolroom—complete with the chanting of multiplication tables.

**Awakening memories** Adults who have never really grown up may well find nostalgic memories of the past. There is a collection of older material such as Victorian dolls and German automata, but probably the best part is recognizing the objects from your own childhood, such as Meccano. If you have children, then a visit will be enjoyable but even without children, this museum should still be on the 'must visit' list.

**Founding father** Patrick Murray said that his museum explored a specialized field of social history. From the early days of the museum he put his own mark on the huge array of exhibits, with his slant on informative labels.

## Calton Hill

**Remarkable buildings grace the top of this volcanic hill, and it is also worth the climb for superb views over the city—Robert Louis Stevenson's most-loved vista of Edinburgh.**

**Grandiose style** Calton Hill (108m/354ft) was known as the Athens of the North in 18th century Edinburgh. This reputation reached almost absurd proportions when a reproduction of the Parthenon was planned, as a memorial to the Scots killed in the Napoleonic Wars. Work began in 1822, but it is said that the money ran out in 1829 and, with only 12 columns completed, the prolific Edinburgh architect William Playfair's grandiose monument became known as 'Edinburgh's Disgrace'. The remaining folly, however, is part of the distinctive skyline of Calton Hill.

**Other monuments** Sharing the slopes of Calton Hill with the National Monument are the Old Observatory (the only surviving building by New Town planner James Craig), and the City Observatory built in 1818, which has exhibitions and viewings of the night sky. Also on the hill is the 1816 tower of the Nelson Monument (Apr–end Sep Mon 1–6, Tue–Sat 10–6; Oct–end Mar Mon–Sat 10–3), a 143-step climb, but worth the effort for a wider view.

**Check out the views** The climb to the windy park at the top is rewarded by superb views. Here on the grassy slopes you can see south to the red-toned cliffs of Salisbury Crags and down to undulating slopes of Holyrood Park or to the east beyond Princes Street. Despite its grand Classical structures, Calton Hill is still very much revered as common ground to many locals and they most certainly want to keep it that way.

### HIGHLIGHTS

- Spectacular views
- Nelson Monument
- National Monument
- City Observatory
- Playfair Monument

### INFORMATION

- G7; Locator map D2
- X26
- Edinburgh Waverley
- For information: Edinburgh Lothian Tourist Information Centre, 3 Princes Street EH2 2QP
- ☎ 0131 473 3800

*The Dugald Stewart Memorial on Calton Hill*

## Canongate Tolbooth

- The building
- Prison cell
- 1940s kitchen
- Cooper's workshop
- Re-created pub

*The turreted steeple of the Tolbooth*

### INFORMATION

www.cac.org.uk

- G8; Locator map D3
- 163 Canongate EH8 8BN
- 0131 529 4057
- Mon–Sat 10–5; also Sun 12–5 in Aug
- 35
- Edinburgh Waverley
- Good
- Free
- Royal Mile (➤ 37), Scottish Parliament Building (➤ 45), Dynamic Earth (➤ 46), Palace of Holyroodhouse (➤ 48)
- Shop stocks a wide range of local social history books

**Dating from 1591, this French-style Tolbooth has served as both a council chamber and a prison. It now houses The People's Story, a museum of everyday life since the 18th century.**

**From toll-house to museum** Just up the hill from the Canongate Kirk, the oldest remaining building in this district was built as a toll-house to mark the boundary between Holyrood and Edinburgh proper. The Tolbooth served as the council chamber for the independent burgh of Canongate until its incorporation into the city in 1856. A five-floor building with a turreted steeple, it was also used as a prison for the burgh. The huge boxed clock that projects above the street was added in 1884.

**Edinburgh life** The building is now home to The People's Story, a museum dedicated to everyday life and times in Edinburgh from the 18th century up to the present day. Using oral history, written sources and the reminiscences of local people, it creates a fascinating insight. Indulge your senses through the visual displays, sounds and smells that evoke life in a prison cell, a draper's shop, a cooper's (barrel maker) workshop. See a servant at work and a tramcar conductor (a 'clippie', who clipped the tickets). The Museum portrays the struggle for improved conditions, better health and ways to enjoy what little leisure the citizens had. There is strong representation from the trades union movement and friendly societies in the struggle for people's rights.

**Time off** Check out the places the locals went for a gossip, such as the re-created pub, the tea room and the wash-house.

## Scottish Parliament Building

**With the passing of the Scotland Act in 1998, the first Scottish Parliament since 1707 was established. After five years in temporary accommodation, it is now in a striking new home.**

**Setting the scene** From 1999, the Scottish Parliament was housed in buildings around the Royal Mile. Debating took place in the Church of Scotland Assembly at the top of The Mound. The then First Minister Donald Dewar commissioned a new parliament building to be constructed opposite Holyrood Palace. At an original estimated cost of around £40 million, the building was finally opened by the Queen in October 2004, by which time the cost had soared to over £400 million. This expense caused a good deal of controversy but the resulting building has also attracted much praise.

**No expense spared** Hailed by architects and critics as one of the most significant new buildings in Britain, the complex was the work of Barcelona-based architect Enric Miralles. It is a unique Catalan-Scottish blend. The building is set within newly landscaped public gardens near the Palace of Holyroodhouse, against a backdrop of the Salisbury Crags. It is designed to complement the listed building Queensberry House. Natural materials have been carefully crafted to produce a fine level of excellence, with expert use of wood, stone and glass. Intricate details in oak and sycamore have been used throughout to offset the granite and smooth concrete finishes. The Debating Chamber, where the 129 members meet, has a striking oak beamed ceiling. Miralles' expertise combined design with practicality through acute attention to detail.

### HIGHLIGHTS

- ● Architecture
- ● Exhibition on Scottish Parliament
- ● Public Gallery

### INFORMATION

**www**.scottish.parliament.uk

⊞ H8; Locator map E3

✉ The Scottish Parliament, Holyrood Road, EH99 1SP

☎ 0131 348 5200

🕐 Business days Tue–Thu 9–7. Non-business days (Mon, Fri and weekends) and when Parliament is in recess Apr–end Oct 10–6; Nov–end Mar 10–4

🍴 Café

▣ 35

🚇 Edinburgh Waverley

♿ Excellent

🎫 Free; tours moderate

🔄 Our Dynamic Earth (➤ 46), Holyrood Park (➤ 47), Palace of Holyroodhouse (➤ 48)

❓ Guided tours lasting 45 minutes are available on most non-business days. Reserve tickets for the Public Gallery in advance. Shop sells exclusive items branded to the Scottish Parliament

Above: *The members' entrance to the Scottish Parliament Building*

45

# Our Dynamic Earth

## HIGHLIGHTS

- Striking building
- Time machine
- Virtual reality helicopter trip
- Tropical rainforest
- 'Submarine trip'
- Restless Earth experience

## INFORMATION

www.dynamicearth.co.uk

🔠 H9; Locator map E3

✉ 112 Holyrood Road
EH8 8AS

☎ 0131 550 7800

*The Polar Gallery*

🕐 Mar–end Oct daily 10–6;
Nov–end Feb Wed–Sun
10–5

🍴 The Food Chain

🚻 35

🚉 Edinburgh Waverley

♿ Excellent

💷 Expensive

↔ Scottish Parliament
Building (► 45),
Holyrood Park (► 47),
Palace of Holyroodhouse
(► 48)

❓ Well-stocked themed
gift shop

**This tented, spiky roof rising like a white armadillo on the edge of Holyrood Park is Edinburgh's Millennium project: a science park that thrills at every turn.**

**Popular science** This interactive spectacular tells the story of the Earth and its changing nature, from the so-called Big Bang (as viewed from the bridge of a space ship) to the present day (exactly who lives where in the rainforest). This is virtual reality at its slickest—great entertainment for kids but it may prove a bit too whizzy for some.

**Stunning effects** With 11 galleries devoted to the planet, the underlying message is that the world is a fascinating and ever-changing place. Experience the effect of erupting volcanoes, the icy chill of the polar regions and even a simulated earthquake while lava apparently boils below. You may get caught in a humid rain storm in the Tropical Rainforest. Every 15 minutes the sky darkens, lightning flashes, thunder roars and torrential rain descends. You can travel in the Time Machine, where numerous stars are created using lights and mirrors. A multi-screen flight over mountains and glaciers is a dizzying highlight.

**Plenty of stamina** Opened in July 1999 close to the new Scottish Parliament building, Our Dynamic Earth is proving a popular, impressive feat of high-tech ingenuity. Although it is hardly a relaxing experience, Our Dynamic Earth is well worth a visit, although peak times are likely to be very crowded.

# Holyrood Park

**It's unusual—and a pleasant surprise—to discover a city park containing such wild countryside. You'll even find whole lochs within Edinburgh's Holyrood Park.**

**City's green treasure** A royal park since the 12th century, Holyrood Park was enclosed by a stone boundary wall in 1541. Spreading out behind the Palace of Holyroodhouse (► 48), it extends to some 263ha (650 acres) and is dominated by the great extinct volcano, Arthur's Seat (► 49). It represents a microcosm of Scottish landscape, boasting four lochs, open moorland, marshes, glens and dramatic cliffs, the Salisbury Crags, a popular spot for rock climbers and abseilers to practise their skills.

**Get your boots on** The park is circled by Queen's Drive, built at the instigation of Prince Albert and closed to commercial vehicles. The headquarters of Holyrood Park Ranger Service is in Queen's Drive and you can pick up maps of walks or find out about the ranger-led walks. The area around Dunsapie Loch gives a real sense of remote countryside, and is a good spot to make the ascent to Arthur's Seat. It is particularly peaceful here when cars are prohibited on Sundays. Altogether Holyrood Park is an excellent place to walk, cycle or picnic.

**More to see** Also in the park is St. Margaret's Well, a medieval Gothic structure near the palace, where a clear spring wells from beneath sculpted vaulting. Above St. Margaret's Loch, a 19th-century artificial lake, are the remains of St. Anthony's Chapel. On the edge of the park you will find Duddingston village, with one of the oldest pubs in Edinburgh and the attractive Duddingston Loch.

## HIGHLIGHTS

● Arthur's Seat
● Dunsapie Loch
● St. Margaret's Well

## INFORMATION

www.historic-scotland.gov.uk
✚ H8–K11; Locator map E3–F4
✉ Holyrood Park
☎ Historic Scotland Ranger Service: 0131 652 8150
🕐 24 hours, 365 days a year, but no vehicular access to Dunsapie Loch on Sun
🚌 35 to palace entrance; other buses to perimeter
🚇 Edinburgh Waverley
♿ Varies, phone for details. Good to Education Centre
💷 Free
🔄 Our Dynamic Earth (► 46), Palace of Holyroodhouse (► 48), Arthur's Seat (► 49)
❓ Maps of walks from the Holyrood Park Ranger Service, Education Centre, 1 Queen's Drive 🕐 Daily 8–4; closes 3.30 Fri

*The park is an important Fringe venue*

# Palace of Holyroodhouse

- State apartments
- Queen's Gallery
- Chambers of Mary, Queen of Scots

## INFORMATION

**www.royal.gov.uk**

- H8; Locator map E3
- Canongate, Royal Mile EH8 8DX
- 0131 556 5100
- Apr–end Oct daily 9.30–6; Nov–end Mar 9.30–4.30. May close at short notice
- Café in old coach house
- 35
- Edinburgh Waverley
- Good
- Expensive
- Royal Mile (► 37), Scottish Parliament Building (► 45), Our Dynamic Earth (► 46), Holyrood Park (► 47), Arthur's Seat (► 49)
- Free audio tour available. Gift shop stocks cards, books and china

*Holyroodhouse sits beneath Arthur's Seat*

**Founded as a monastery in 1128, today the palace is the Queen's official residence in Scotland. It is set against the backdrop of majestic Arthur's Seat, at the foot of the Royal Mile.**

**Steeped in royal history** In the 15th century the palace became a guest house for the neighbouring Holyrood Abbey (now a scenic ruin), and its name is said to derive from the Holy Rood, a fragment of Christ's Cross belonging to David I (c.1080–1153). Mary, Queen of Scots, stayed here, and a brass plate marks where her Italian favourite, David Rizzio, was murdered in her private apartments in the west tower in 1566. During the Civil War in 1650 the palace was seriously damaged by fire and major rebuilding was necessary. Bonnie Prince Charlie held court here in 1745, followed by George IV on his triumphant visit to the city in 1822, and later by Queen Victoria en route to Balmoral.

**Home and art gallery** The palace offers all the advantages of exploring a living space steeped in history and filled with works of art from the Royal Collection. More precious artworks are on view in the stunning Queen's Gallery, by the entrance and opposite the new Scottish Parliament. The state rooms, designed by architect William Bruce (1630–1710) and hung with Brussels tapestries, are particularly splendid. Don't miss the preposterous royal portraits painted in a hurry by Jacob de Wet in 1684–86, which are hung in the Great Gallery.

**Phone ahead** The palace is closed to visitors whenever a member of the royal family is in residence and security surrounding the building is very tight.

## Arthur's Seat

**The perfect antidote to the stresses of the city, with spectacular views. Arthur's Seat is the remains of an extinct volcano 325 million years old, and it's right on Edinburgh's doorstep.**

**Geological background**  The green hill of Arthur's Seat is a city landmark, 251m (823ft) high and visible for miles. Formed during the early Carboniferous era, it is surrounded by seven smaller hills. The summit marks where the cone erupted and molten rock from the volcano formed the high cliffs of Salisbury Crags. During the Ice Age erosion exposed the twin peaks of Arthur's Seat and the Crow Hill. There are a variety of explanations for the name; some say it is a corruption of the Gaelic name for 'archers', others that the Normans associated it with King Arthur.

**Get active**  There is open access to Arthur's Seat, the hills and four small lochs, all of which are part of the Royal Park of Holyrood. It is worth the climb to the top for the views over the Palace of Holyroodhouse and beyond. Start your climb from a path near St. Margaret's Well, just inside the palace's entrance to the park. The path divides at the start of Hunter's Bog valley but both branches lead to the summit. The right-hand path will take you along the Radical Road that runs beneath the rock face of the Salisbury Crags. The left path goes through Piper's Walk to the top. You'll find parking at the palace, in Duddingston village and by the pools of St. Margaret's Loch and Dunsapie Loch, which has a bird reserve. From the loch it is just a short climb over some rocks to the top. From here the whole panorama of Edinburgh is beneath you, plus the Firth of Forth, the Pentland hills and the coast.

**HIGHLIGHTS**

- Spectacular views
- The walk to the top
- Dunsapie Loch and bird reserve

**INFORMATION**

- 🚌 J10; Locator map F4
- ✉ Holyrood Park
- ⏰ 24 hours, 365 days, but no vehicular access to Dunsapie Loch on Sun
- 🚌 35 and then walk through park; or 4, 5, 44, 45 to Meadowbank and walk
- 🚆 Edinburgh Waverley
- ♿ Few

*A view of the city from the summit*

- 🎟 Free
- ❓ Allow 45 minutes to 2 hours to walk from the palace; take food and drink and be aware weather can change quickly. The walk from the car park at Dunsapie Loch takes 20 minutes
- 🔁 Our Dynamic Earth (➤ 46), Holyrood Park (➤ 47), Palace of Holyroodhouse (➤ 48)

# Craigmillar Castle

## HIGHLIGHTS

- Views
- Substantial ruins
- Queen Mary's Room
- Former chapel and dovecote

## INFORMATION

www.historic-scotland.gov.uk
- M14; Locator map off E4
- Craigmillar Castle Road EH16 4SY
- 0131 661 4445
- Apr–end Sep daily 9.30–6.30; Oct–end Mar Mon–Wed and Sat 9.30–4.30, Thu 9.30–noon, Sun 2–4.30
- 2, 14
- Poor, but access to visitor centre
- Moderate

**The ruins of one of Scotland's most impressive 15th-century tower houses are particularly pleasant to visit when the hustle and bustle of Edinburgh becomes too much.**

**Splendid remains** Craigmillar lies 4km (2.5 miles) southeast of the heart of the city, off the A7, and is often overlooked in favour of the more famous Edinburgh Castle. It is reached via some of Edinburgh's less-admired housing developments, but it's worth the effort. At its core is a well-preserved early 15th-century L-plan tower house with walls up to 2.7m (9ft) thick, constructed on the site of an older fortification by Sir George Preston. His grandson, William, added the curtain wall in the 1440s. The main defensive features include massive doors, a spiral turnpike stair (connecting three floors), narrow passageways and two outer walls to fend off English attackers.

**Fit for a queen** Mary, Queen of Scots, fled here on several occasions when the pressures of life at Holyrood became too great, notably after the murder of her secretary and favourite David Rizzio in 1566, and the tiny chamber where she slept bears her name. It is said that during this stay consipirators agreed to the 'Craigmillar Bond', the plot to kill Lord Darnley, Mary's unpopular husband.

**Falls into ruin** Craigmillar was bought from the Preston family by Sir John Gilmour with the intention to convert it into a fashionable residence. The family, however, decided to move to Inch House at Gilmerton instead and Craigmillar was abandoned. Overgrown and ruinous, it was acquired by the state in 1946. Today it is in the hands of Historic Scotland.

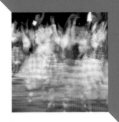

# EDINBURGH's
## best

# Buildings, Churches & Monuments

### SCOTTISH NATIONAL WAR MEMORIAL

Located within the walls of Edinburgh Castle (➤ 31), the memorial was designed by Sir Robert Latimer in 1923–28 to honour the 150,000 Scots who died in World War I. A further 50,000 victims' names from World War II were later added.

*Canongate Kirk, topped by a gilded stag's head*

*The Heart of Midlothian commemorates the site of public executions*

### ASSEMBLY ROOMS

Even if you're not attending a concert here, it's worth visiting to admire the elegance of the rooms, which opened in 1787. Take in the ballroom, with its dazzling chandeliers, and the huge music hall.

➕ E8  ✉ 54 George Street EH2 2LE  ☎ 0131 220 4349  🕐 Mon–Sat 10–5  🚌 19, 36, 37, 41  🚉 Edinburgh Waverley  ♿ Good  💷 Varies for performances

### CANONGATE KIRK

Built in 1688, this church's distinctive Dutch gable and plain interior reflect the Canongate's trading links with the Low Countries. Note the gilded stag's head at the gable top, traditionally a gift of the monarch. Buried in the graveyard are the economist and philosopher Adam Smith (1723–90) and David Rizzio, favourite of Mary, Queen of Scots, murdered in 1566.

➕ G8  ✉ Canongate EH8 8BR  ☎ 0131 556 3515  🕐 Jun–end Sep Mon–Sat 10.30–4, Sun 10–12.30; burial ground open all year  ♿ Good  🚌 35  🚉 Edinburgh Waverley  💷 Free

### HEART OF MIDLOTHIAN

With your back to the entrance of St. Giles' Cathedral, move 20 paces forward and slightly to the right, look down and you will see the outline of a heart in the cobblestones. This Heart of Midlothian marks the place of the old Tolbooth prison, where executions took place. Local custom is to spit on this spot!

➕ F9  ✉ High Street EH1 1RE  ☎ 0131 556 3515  🚌 35  🚉 Edinburgh Waverley

### HOLYROOD ABBEY

You can see the ruins of the abbey only on a visit to the Palace of Holyroodhouse (➤ 48). The original abbey was founded by David I for the Augustinians, but the present structure was built in the early 13th century. It was sacked by the English in 1547 and partially destroyed after the Reformation.

➕ H8  ✉ The Palace of Holyroodhouse EH8 8DX  ☎ 0131 556 5100  🕐 Apr–end Oct daily 9.30–6; Nov–end Mar 9.30–4.30. May close at short notice  🚌 35  🚉 Edinburgh Waverley  ♿ Good  💷 Expensive

## LAURISTON CASTLE

This 'castle' is the epitome of Edwardian comfort and style, a gabled and turreted mansion in a leafy setting overlooking the Firth of Forth near Cramond. Starting out as a simple tower house, Lauriston was remodelled and extended several times. The castle was left to the City of Edinburgh in 1926 by William Robert Reid, a wealthy business owner and avid collector of furniture and objets d'art.

➕ Off map at A4 ✉ 2A Cramond Road South, Davidson's Mains EH4 5QD ☎ 0131 336 2060 ⏰ Apr–end Oct Sat–Thu tours every hour 11.20–4.20; Nov–end Mar Sat–Sun at 2.20 and 3.20. Grounds open 9am–dusk 🚌 24 ♿ Good 💷 Castle: moderate. Grounds: free

## MERCAT CROSS

Located outside St. Giles' Cathedral, the cross was traditionally the chosen location for public declarations, gatherings and executions. The present version, dating from the 1880s, is modelled on the 17th-century cross. There may have been a cross here since the 12th century, when it was a focus for trade.

➕ F9 ✉ High Street 🚌 23, 27, 35, 41 🚉 Edinburgh Waverley

## PARLIAMENT HOUSE

The heart of the Scottish legal system, occupied by the law courts. Dating from the 17th century, it has a fine old hammerbeam roof and a lovely 19th-century stained-glass window. It was home to Parliament from 1639 to 1707 and again from 1999 to 2004.

➕ F9 ✉ Parliament Square EH1 1RF ☎ 0131 225 2595 ⏰ Mon–Fri 9–5 🚌 23, 27, 35, 41 🚉 Edinburgh Waverley ♿ Good 💷 Free

## REAL MARY KING'S CLOSE

Remnants of 17th-century houses, part of the rabbit warren of the Old Town, have been preserved beneath the City Chamber, which was built over the top in 1753. Archaeological research in 2002–3 showed evidence of the people who lived here up until the 20th century. Guided tours underground bring the close and its people to life.

➕ F9 ✉ 2 Warriston's Close, High Street EH1 1PG ☎ 0870 243 0160 ⏰ Apr–end Oct daily 10–9; Nov–end Mar 10–4 🚌 23, 27, 35, 41 🚉 Edinburgh Waverley ♿ Few, phone for details 💷 Expensive

## REGISTER HOUSE

Register House was originally sited in the castle and then in the Tolbooth. In 1774 a custom-built Register House in Princes Street was designed by Robert Adam to house the national archives. Still in use today, it is guarded by a famous statue of Wellington.

➕ F8 ✉ Scottish Record Office, 2 Princes Street EH1 3YT ☎ 0131 535 1314 ⏰ Mon–Fri 9–4.30 🚉 Edinburgh Waverley ♿ Good 💷 Free

*Lauriston Castle has fine Edwardian interiors*

### ST. MARY'S EPISCOPAL CATHEDRAL

It was William Walker's unmarried daughters, Barbara and Mary, who bequeathed a legacy to build this cathedral. St. Mary's, with the sisters' mansion house still in its shadow, is a Gothic creation with a central tower rising to 84m (276ft). It was designed by Sir Gilbert Scott and built between 1874 and 1879. There are some interesting murals inside by one of the leading lights of the Arts and Crafts movement, Phoebe Anna Traquair. The twin western towers, known affectionately as Barbara and Mary, were added in 1917.

➕ C9 ✉ Palmerston Place EH12 5AW ☎ 0131 225 6293 ⏰ Mon–Fri 7.30–6, Sat, Sun 7.30–5 🚌 2, 25, 31, 44 ♿ Very good

# Museums

## JOHN KNOX HOUSE

Whether the great reformer actually lived in this house is uncertain, but he certainly used to preach from the front window. Dating back to the 1490s, the house is typical of the period, with overhanging gables and picturesque windows. Housed within is a museum with displays relating to Knox and to James Mosman, jeweller to Mary, Queen of Scots. The house is also home to the Scottish Storytelling Centre (➤ 83).

➕ G9 ✉ 43–45 High Street EH1 1SR ☎ 0131 556 9579 🕐 Mon–Sat 10–4.30 🚌 35 and all North Bridge buses

*John Knox House was originally two houses*

## BANK OF SCOTLAND MUSEUM

Located in the bank's headquarters, this small, unusual museum displays old maps, prints, gold coins, banknotes, forgeries, bullion chests and more.

➕ E9 ✉ Bank of Scotland Head Office, The Mound, Edinburgh EH1 1YZ ☎ 0131 529 1288 🕐 Mid-Jun to early Sep Mon–Fri 10–4.45; otherwise by appointment 🚌 23, 27, 41, 42 🚉 Edinburgh Waverley ♿ Good 💷 Free

## CAMERA OBSCURA

You'll find the Camera Obscura at the top of the Royal Mile in a castellated building known as the Outlook Tower. The camera obscura, invented in the 19th century, is like a giant pin-hole camera, with no film involved. It projects onto a viewing table a fascinating panorama of the city outside. Take a look through the Superscope, the most powerful telescope in Britain. It's best to visit on a clear day.

➕ E9 ✉ Castlehill EH1 2ND ☎ 0131 226 3709 🕐 Jul–end Aug daily 9.30–7.30; Apr–end Jun, Sep–end Oct 9.30–6; Nov–end Mar 10–5 🚌 23, 27, 35, 41, 42 🚉 Edinburgh Waverley ♿ None 💷 Free

## GLADSTONE'S LAND

This highlight in the Old Town is the re-creation of a 17th-century tenement. It emphasizes the cramped Old Town conditions—the only space for expansion was upwards and the building's eventual height of six floors reflects the status of its merchant owner, Thomas Gledstanes, who extended the existing tenement in 1617. The National Trust for Scotland has re-created 17th-century shop-booths on the ground floor, where there are original painted ceilings, adorned with flowers and birds.

➕ F9 ✉ 477b Lawnmarket EH1 2NT ☎ 0131 226 5856 🕐 Apr–end Oct Mon–Sat, Sun 2–5 🚌 2, 23, 27, 35, 41, 42 🚉 Edinburgh Waverley ♿ None 💷 Moderate

## MUSEUM OF EDINBURGH

The home of Edinburgh's own museum is Huntly House, a 16th-

century dwelling much altered in subsequent centuries and at one time occupied by a trade guild, the Incorporation of Hammermen. The collections relate to the history of Edinburgh and include maps and prints, silver, glass and old shop signs, and Greyfriars Bobby's collar. Also on show is the original National Covenant signed in 1638.

🔢 G9 ✉ Huntly House, 142 Canongate, Royal Mile EH8 8DD ☎ 0131 529 4143 🕐 Mon–Sat 10–5; also Sun 2–5 during Aug 🚻 Poor 🎫 Free 🚌 35 🚇 Edinburgh Waverley

### NATIONAL WAR MUSEUM OF SCOTLAND
Exploring more than 400 years of Scottish military history in the imposing setting of Edinburgh Castle, this museum has displays ranging from major events in Scottish warfare down to the personal—diaries, private photographs and belongings of ordinary soldiers. Highlights include a pipe given by a German soldier to a sergeant in the Scots Guards on Christmas Day 1914; a vast array of weaponry; gallantry medals; and even three elephant's toes.

🔢 E9 ✉ Edinburgh Castle, Castle Hill EH1 2NG ☎ 0131 247 4413 🕐 Daily 9.45–5.45 (closes 4.45 Nov–end Mar) 🚻 Good 🎫 Expensive (as part of ticket for castle) 🚌 23, 27, 35, 41 🚇 Edinburgh Waverly

### TRON KIRK
This fine early Scottish Renaissance church was built between 1637 and 1663 and stands on the Royal Mile. Its name derives from the salt-tron, a public weighbeam that once stood outside. The church has not been used for public worship since 1952 and now houses the Old Town Information Centre.

🔢 F9 ✉ High Street EH1 2NG ☎ 0131 225 8408 🕐 Apr–end Oct daily 10–5.30; Nov–end Mar daily 12–5 🚌 35 and all North Bridge buses 🚇 Edinburgh Waverley 🚻 Poor, steps into church 🎫 Free

### THE WRITERS' MUSEUM
The narrow 17th-century Lady Stair's House is home to the Writers' Museum and dedicated notably to Robert Burns (1759–96), Walter Scott (1771–1832) and Robert Louis Stevenson (1850–94). Scott and Stevenson were both born in Edinburgh, and both studied law at the university. Particularly significant is Stevenson's memorabilia, as he died abroad and there is no other museum dedicated to him. Contemporary Scottish authors are also represented.

🔢 F9 ✉ Lady Stair's Close, Lawnmarket, Royal Mile EH1 2PA ☎ 0131 529 4901 🕐 Mon–Sat 10–5; also Sun 2–5 in Aug 🚌 35 🚇 Edinburgh Waverley 🚻 Phone for details 🎫 Free

### PEOPLE'S WAR AT EDINBURGH CASTLE

The new permanent exhibition at Edinburgh Castle (➤ 31) is proving a resounding success. Two hundred years of old graffiti in the prison vaults has been the inspiration behind the re-creation of life for prisoners in the late 18th century. Hundreds of captured foreign sailors were incarcerated here. As well as carvings of ships on the prison doors, many carefully crafted objects, including model ships made by the prisoners, are on display.

*Above left: A brass sculpture from the exterior of Gladstone's Land*

*The painted ceiling in Gladstone's Land main bedroom*

# Edinburgh's Best

# Galleries

*The North Door of the Royal Scottish Academy*

### WESTON LINK

The £30 million project providing an underground link between the Royal Scottish Academy and the National Gallery of Scotland was opened in August 2004. Providing two extra galleries for changing exhibitions, it will display art in one of the finest spaces anywhere in the world. The building is flooded with light from Princes Street Gardens. Facilities include a 200-seat lecture theatre and cinema, a large restaurant, café and shop.

### CITY ART CENTRE

Established in 1980, the gallery is housed in a six-floor former warehouse. It stages changing exhibitions and displays the city's collection of Scottish paintings, including works by the 20th-century Scottish Colourists.

➕ F9 ✉ 2 Market Street EH1 1DE ☎ 0131 529 3993 ⏰ Mon–Sat 10–5, also Sun 12–5 Aug 🚌 23, 27, 41 🚉 Edinburgh Waverley ♿ Very good 🎟 Free; charge for some exhibitions

### DEAN GALLERY

Across the road from the Scottish National Gallery of Modern Art, this gallery is housed in a former orphanage and displays an excellent collection based around the work of Dada and the Surrealists, and the Scottish sculptor Eduardo Palozzi (b.1924).

➕ B8 ✉ 73 Belford Road EH4 13DS ☎ 0131 624 6200 ⏰ Daily 10–5, Thu until 7 🚌 13; free bus linking main galleries 🚉 Edinburgh Haymarket ♿ Very good 🎟 Free; charge for some exhibitions

### ROYAL SCOTTISH ACADEMY

William Playfair's lovely Classical building has been fully restored and is now linked to the National Gallery to create a superb space for displaying art.

➕ E8 ✉ The Mound EH2 2EL ☎ 0131 624 6200 ⏰ Daily 10–5, Thu until 7 🚌 3, 10, 17, 23, 24, 27, 44; free bus linking main galleries 🚉 Edinburgh Waverley ♿ Very good 🎟 Free; charge for some exhibitions

### SCOTTISH NATIONAL PORTRAIT GALLERY

This gallery tells the history of Scotland through the portraits of the great and the good, the bad, the beautiful and the vain. A host of familiar faces include the original and much copied portrait of poet Robert Burns by Alexander Nasmyth (1758–1840).

➕ F7 ✉ 1 Queen Street EH2 1JD ☎ 0131 624 6200 ⏰ Daily 10–5, Thu until 7 🚌 8, 23, 27; free bus linking main galleries 🚉 Edinburgh Waverley ♿ Very good 🎟 Free; charge for some exhibitions

### TALBOT RICE GALLERY

Within the University of Edinburgh, this gallery was established in 1975 and hosts changing exhibitions showcasing Scottish art and the work of international artists. There is also the fine permanent Torrie collection of Dutch and Italian Old Masters.

➕ F9 ✉ Old College, South Bridge EH8 9YL ☎ 0131 650 2210 ⏰ Tue–Sat 10–5; daily during Festival 🚌 3, 7, 8, 14, 33 🚉 Edinburgh Waverley ♿ Good 🎟 Free; charge for some exhibitions

# Statues

### ALLAN RAMSAY

In the West Princes Street Gardens is a statue of the former wig-maker turned poet, Allan Ramsay (1684–1758). His best known work, The Gentle Shepherd, was an instant success. The statue, carved by Sir John Steel, was erected in 1865.

➕ D9–E9 ✉ West Princes Street Gardens 🚌 3, 10, 17, 23, 24, 27

### CHARLES II

This splendid memorial to Charles II (1630–85) is the oldest statue in Edinburgh and the oldest equestrian statue in Britain. Made of lead, it was designed by an unknown sculptor and erected in 1685.

➕ F9 ✉ Parliament Square 🚌 23, 27, 35, 41

### DAVID LIVINGSTONE

Close to the Scott Monument is a bronze statue of the 19th-century missionary and explorer David Livingstone (1813–73). The piece was sculpted by Amelia Robertson Hill in 1876.

➕ F8 ✉ East Princes Street Gardens 🚌 3, 10, 17, 23, 24, 27, 44

### THE DUKE OF WELLINGTON

Outside Register House in Princes Street, this 12-ton bronze equestrian statue of Arthur Wellesley, 1st Duke of Wellington (1769–1852), was designed by Sir John Steel. Remarkably, the entire weight of the sculpture rests on the horse's hind legs and tail.

➕ F8 ✉ Princes Street 🚌 8, 25, 29, 37

### HENRY DUNDAS, FIRST VISCOUNT MELVILLE

The Melville Monument stands 41m (134ft) high, in the middle of St. Andrew Square. There is a good view of the statue from the end of George Street. Viscount Melville (1742–1811) was so influential in Scottish politics he was nicknamed 'the uncrowned King of Scotland'.

➕ F8 ✉ St. Andrew Square 🚌 8, 12, 17

### JOHN KNOX

The founder of the Church of Scotland, Knox (*c*1505–72) was minister at St. Giles' Cathedral from 1559 and is buried in the churchyard. His statue stands against the wall of St. Giles, designed by MacGillivray in 1906.

➕ F9 ✉ Parliament Square 🚌 23, 27, 35, 41

### MORE STATUES

There are more than 200 statues and monuments in and around Edinburgh. Look out for Robert the Bruce (on the left) and William Wallace (on the right), guarding the entrance to Edinburgh Castle. At the bottom of Castlehill is a striking equestrian statue of Field Marshal Earl Haig. Spot the equestrian statue of the Scots Grey Guards soldier on Princes Street. In Picardy Place is the only statue in Britain of the famous fictional detective, Sherlock Holmes. Out at Leith you will find a bronze statue of the Scottish bard Robert Burns in Bernard Street.

Above: *Robert Burns.*
Left: *John Knox.*
Below: *Robert the Bruce*

# Parks & Open Spaces

### VIEWS

Edinburgh has some of the best views and vantage points of any city in Europe. The most rewarding are from the top of Arthur's Seat (➤ 49), the ramparts of Edinburgh Castle (➤ 31), from Calton Hill (➤ 43), the Scott Monument (➤ 35) and the roof terrace at the Museum of Scotland (➤ 39). Great views of the Royal Mile can be seen when you stand on the corner of Lawnmarket and the High Street. Take time to pause in New Town to absorb the amazing grandeur of Georgian town planning. Farther out at South Queensferry you can get a good view of the two Forth bridges from below.

### BLACKFORD HILL

One of Edinburgh's seven hills, the view from here in all directions is excellent. Just 3km (2 miles) south of central Edinburgh, it is home to the Royal Scottish Observatory, which moved here from Calton Hill in 1895. The visitor centre is open only for group visits and occasional events. There are Friday evening viewing sessions in winter that must be booked in advance (☎ 0131 668 8404).

✚ E15 ⊠ Blackford 🚌 24, 38, 41 ♿ Few

### BRAID HILLS

Lying a few miles south of Blackford Hill, it is possible to walk from here along good paths to Blackford. The views across the city are spectacular and you can get one of the best views of the Forth bridges on a clear day. Golf courses dominate the area.

✚ Off map at C15 ⊠ Braid Hills ☎ 0131 529 3993 🚌 11, 24, 38 ♿ Few

### CORSTORPHINE HILL

If you visit Edinburgh Zoo (➤ 26) you might like to carry on up to the summit of Corstophine Hill (160m/525ft). Here you will find Clermiston Tower, erected in 1871 to the memory of Sir Walter Scott.

✚ Off map A10 ⊠ Corstorphine Hill 🚌 12, 26, 31 ♿ Good

### THE MEADOWS

Paths and tree-planted areas make this an ideal place to wander away from the hustle of the city; although not such a good place to be at night. Very much a local's hangout—students from the university, doctors and nurses from the nearby Royal Infirmary and families from the surrounding district all mingle here. It has a children's playground.

✚ D11–E11 ⊠ The Meadows 🚌 5, 7, 11, 31 ♿ Good

*Dean village is on the banks of the Water of Leith*

### WATER OF LEITH

This small river meanders gently through Edinburgh suburbs. There is more dramatic scenery at Dean (➤ 60). A riverside walkway, 21km (13 miles) long, stretches from Balerno to Leith with the most scenic stretch centred around Stockbridge (➤ 32).

✚ A9–J2 ⊠ From Balerno to Leith (access at different points) 🚌 2, 23, 27 ♿ Few. Visitor Centre: ⊠ 24 Lanark Road (near Balerno) ☎ 0131 455 7367 🕐 Apr–end Sep daily 10–4; Oct–end Mar Wed–Sun 10–4 🚌 44 🎟 Inexpensive to interactive exhibition

# For Children

### BRASS RUBBING CENTRE

Great choice of brasses—medieval knights, Pictish symbols and Celtic designs. No experience needed and staff are on hand to help. Equipment is provided.

➕ G9 ✉ Trinity Apse, Chalmers Close, High Street EH1 1SS ☎ 0131 556 4364 🕐 Apr–end Sep Mon–Sat 10–5; also Aug Sun 12–5 🚌 35 and all North Bridge buses 🚉 Edinburgh Waverley ♿ None 💷 Free to centre, small charge for rubbing

### DEEP SEA WORLD

Sited beneath the Forth Rail Bridge, this attraction has one of the largest collections of sand tiger sharks in Europe and a long walk-through underwater tunnel.

➕ Off map at A4 ✉ Battery Quarry, North Queensferry (20 minutes drive from Edinburgh) ☎ 01383 411 880 🕐 Daily 10–6 (closes at 5 Sep–end Mar); Thu until 7 🍴 Lagoon café 🚉 North Queensferry ♿ Very good 💷 Expensive

### THE EDINBURGH DUNGEON

Deep beneath the paving stones of Edinburgh you enter the sinister side of Scotland's past. Encounter witch-hunters, grave-robbers and murderers; expect darkness, skeletons and host of special effects. Not for the faint hearted or very young children.

➕ F9 ✉ 31 Market Street EH1 1QB ☎ 0131 240 1000 🕐 Apr–end Jun, Sep–end Oct daily 10–5; Jul, Aug daily 10–7; Mar 11–4; Nov–end Feb Mon–Fri 11–4, Sat, Sun 10.30–4.30 🚌 All buses to Waverley Station (one-minute walk) 🚉 Edinburgh Waverley ♿ Phone for details 💷 Expensive

### LEITH WATERWORLD

Fun with a splash. Leisure pool, flumes, slides and water features including wave machine, river run, geysers and more. Also a learner pool. Children under eight must be accompanied by an adult.

➕ H4 ✉ 377 Easter Road EH6 8HU ☎ 0131 555 6000 🕐 Christmas, Easter and summer (Jul to mid-Aug) school holidays daily 10.30–4.45; Fri–Sun 10.30–4.45 outside holidays 🚌 1, 35 ♿ Good 💷 Moderate

### TARTAN WEAVING MILL

From sheep to finished garment, learn about the processes of making a kilt—and try the loom.

➕ E9 ✉ 555 Castlehill EH1 2ND ☎ 0131 226 1555 🕐 Daily 9–5.30 🚌 23, 27, 41, 42 🚉 Edinburgh Waverley ♿ Good 💷 Free exhibition; tours (Mon–Fri) moderate

### FRESH AIR FOR FREE

Sightseeing can be very expensive with children. Why not pass some time at Edinburgh's green and pleasant places and allow the kids to let off steam? Let them climb to the top of Arthur's Seat (► 49), Castlehill and Calton Hill (► 43), or take a picnic at St. Margaret's Loch in Holyrood Park (► 47); this is also a great place to feed the ducks, fly kites, throw frisbees or play football.

*Above: Some of the puppets on display at the Museum of Childhood. Below: Face-painting can be fun*

# Villages, Streets & Districts

## EDINBURGH EXCHANGE

A £350-million development scheme was launched in 1988 to rejuvenate this run-down area. So far the scheme has promoted the construction of impressive new buildings such as the Edinburgh International Conference Centre, designed by architect Terry Farrell and opened in 1995. There is still more building on the way to add to the striking modern structures of brick, stone and glass that already exist.
🚩 D10 ⊠ Lothian Road and West Approach Road 🚌 10, 11, 22, 30

*The Edinburgh Exchange is undergoing significant redevelopment*

## ANN STREET

One of Edinburgh's most exclusive addresses is based on the estate built in 1814 by artist Sir Henry Raeburn in memory of his wife, Ann. Located between Stockbridge and New Town, the houses combine classic splendour with cottagey charm.
🚩 C7 ⊠ Ann Street 🚌 29, 37, 41, 42

## CORSTORPHINE

Most people visit Corstorphine on a trip to the zoo (► 26) or to climb to the top of the hill (► 58). However, old Corstorphine, south of the main Glasgow road, is also worth visiting for its attractive church and barrel-shaped dovecote capable of housing 1,600 birds, which used to serve the long-gone castle.
🚩 Off map at A10 ⊠ Corstorphine 🚌 12, 26, 31

## CRAMOND

There are Roman remains, 16th-century houses, a fine church, an old inn and some elegant Victorian villas to hold your attention in this attractive suburb on the shores of the Firth of Forth. The Cramond Trust has a permanent exhibition in the Maltings exploring the history of the village. Take one of the good walks around the area or visit Lauriston Castle (► 53), nearby.
🚩 Off map at A4 ⊠ Cramond 🕐 Maltings Jun–end Sep Sat–Sun 2–5; every afternoon during Festival 🚌 41

## DEAN VILLAGE

The northern limit of New Town is marked by Thomas Telford's 1832 Dean Bridge. It spans a steep gorge created by the Water of Leith. Dean was a successful grain-milling hamlet for more than 800 years with 11 working mills in the area at one time. After a decline in trade, the workers' cottages, warehouses and mill buildings have been restored and Dean has become a desirable residential area. Check out the cemetery, the resting place of many well-known locals, including the New Town architect William Playfair.
🚩 B8–C8 ⊠ Dean 🚌 13, 37, 41

## DUDDINGSTON

A welcome retreat from busy city life, Duddingston, to the east of Holyrood Park, is one of Edinburgh's most

attractive and best-preserved villages. Highlights include the 12th-century Duddingston Kirk, one of the oldest churches in Scotland still in use, and the Sheep Heid Inn, dating from the late 16th century, complete with the oldest skittle alley in Scotland.

➕ Off map M10 ✉ Duddingston 🚌 42, 44, 45

### GRASSMARKET

A long open space below the castle rock, the Grassmarket was first chartered as a market in 1477, with corn and cattle sold here for nearly 300 years. It was also the site of public executions. A stone marks the location of the old gibbet and commemorates the Covenanting martyrs who died here. Smartened up in recent years, it now has many good shops and eating places, and the ancient White Hart Inn.

➕ E9 ✉ Grassmarket 🚌 2, 35

### MORNINGSIDE

Immortalized in the accent of novelist Muriel Spark's Jean Brodie, this southwest suburb still houses the wealthy of the city. A quiet leafy spot graced with Victorian villas, it has oozed respectability for more than a century. Stroll round its pleasant streets and take in a bit of retail therapy and afternoon tea.

➕ D13 ✉ Morningside 🚌 5, 11, 15, 15A, 16, 17, 23, 41

### MURRAYFIELD

Developed around the 18th-century Murrayfield House, this western suburb is a pleasant district and popular with city commuters. Scottish rugby has made its home here and the stadium (➤ 85) hosts games during the Six Nations championships. The stadium was built by the Scottish Football Union and opened in 1925. It has a seating capacity of 67,500.

➕ Off map at A10 ✉ Murrayfield ☎ Murrayfield Stadium 0131 346 5000 ♿ Good 🚌 12, 22, 26, 31

**STOCKBRIDGE** (➤ 32)

*One of Swanston's picturesque thatched cottages*

### SWANSTON

Located on the northern slopes of the Pentland Hills, this village seems a thousand miles away from the city. It is a conservation village, a huddle of 18th-century thatched, whitewashed cottages. One of these, Swanston Cottage, was the holiday home of the Stevenson family, where the sickly Robert Louis spent his summers from 1867 to 1880. The easiest way to visit is by car.

➕ Off map at C15 ✉ Swanston 🚌 5, 27 (check with Lothian Buses), followed by walk

*Murrayfield is home to Scotland's international rugby union team*

# Events

## FESTIVAL TIPS

• Reserve your accommodation well in advance, especially in August when the Tattoo and the Fringe run simultaneously.
• If you're going to the Tattoo some supplies are helpful. Take binoculars, a waterproof, a cushion and a rug—it's often chilly in Scotland even in August.
• Acquaint yourself with the Fringe programme, it's huge but free and lists every show. When reserving tickets see which shows have been selling out as that's an indication it's good.
• To see those faces at the Fringe you've 'seen on TV' try the most likely venues—the Pleasance and the Assembly Rooms on George Street.
• Be daring and try to catch something really different at the Fringe; you never know— you might enjoy it!

## CAPITAL CHRISTMAS

If you're in Edinburgh between the last week in November and 24th December you'll find an action-packed programme of events and attractions. Apart from the usual Christmas lights, there is a traditional German street market, the Edinburgh wheel, giving a chance to view the city from a different perspective, and Winter Wonderland, Britain's largest outdoor ice rink, located in East Princes Street Gardens.
✉ Venues throughout the city  ☎ www.capitalchristmas.co.uk  🕐 Last week in Nov–24th Dec

## EDINBURGH FESTIVAL FRINGE

Anyone who can raise the funds to pay for a venue can join in the Festival, which is the largest arts festival in the world. Amateurs rub shoulders with professionals as Edinburgh transforms into the world's largest stage, with schools, churches, the streets and the parks all becoming venues. The programme comes out in June and tickets go fast for top acts.
✉ Fringe office: 180 High Street EH1 1QSL  ☎ 0131 226 0026; box office 0131 226 0000; www.edinburghfringe.co.uk  🕐 Starts first Sun in Aug and continues for the month

## EDINBURGH HOGMANAY

Scotland's New Year—Hogmanay—eclipses Christmas as a major event, and Edinburgh celebrates it in style. The four-day extravaganza includes concerts, street parties, live music, marching bands, processions and spectacular fireworks at venues all around the city. Even outside the cordoned area there's plenty of choice for revellers.
✉ Venues throughout the city  ☎ www.edinburghshogmanay.org  🕐 Main revels 31 Dec; also other events during the week running up to New Year's Day

## EDINBURGH MILITARY TATTOO

You'll need to book early for this one. The spectacle takes place on the castle Esplanade with military precision—the swirl of the kilts, the sound of the pipes—this is the greatest tattoo of them all.
➕ E9  ✉ Edinburgh Castle EH8 9YL  ☎ Ticket sales 0870 555 118; www.edintattoo.co.uk (on sale from early Mar)  🕐 3 weeks in Aug  🚌 23, 27, 35, 41, 42  🚇 Edinburgh Waverley  💷 Expensive

## ROYAL HIGHLAND SHOW

Four days of livestock judging, show jumping and crafts come together at Scotland's biggest agricultural show.
➕ Off map A4  ✉ Royal Highland Centre, Ingliston EH28 8NF  ☎ 0131 335 6200; www.rhass.org.uk  🕐 End of Jun  🚌 Special buses laid on for show days  💷 Expensive

*Bands parade at the Edinburgh Military Tattoo*

# EDINBURGH
## where to...

### EAT

### SHOP

### BE ENTERTAINED

### STAY

# Scottish Cuisine

## PRICES

Expect to pay per person for a meal, excluding drinks

£ = Up to £12
££ = £12– £25
£££ = Over £25

## TIPS FOR EATING OUT

Many Edinburgh restaurants can seat customers who walk in off the street, but if you have your heart set on eating at a particular establishment reserve a table in advance. Most restaurants are happy to serve a one- or- two course meal, if that is all you want. If you pay by credit card, when you sign the receipt it may include a section to add a tip. It's acceptable to ignore this and leave a cash tip instead. The normal amount, assuming you are happy with the service, is about 10–15 per cent. In Edinburgh it is fairly common for a reservation to last only a couple of hours, after which time you will be expected to vacate the table to make way for the next sitting.

### ATRIUM (££)

A popular sophisticated eatery in the heart of theatreland that prides itself on a distinctive range of imaginative Scottish dishes.
➕ D9 ✉ 10 Cambridge Street EH1 2ED ☎ 0131 228 8882 🕓 Lunch, dinner; closed Sun, lunch Sat (except Aug) 🚌 10, 11, 16, 22

### DUBH PRAIS RESTAURANT (££)

A truly Scottish restaurant serving the best produce—haggis, beef, lamb, venison and salmon—in its small cellar dining room, well placed on Edinburgh's Royal Mile.
➕ F9 ✉ 123b High Street EH1 1SG ☎ 0131 557 5732 🕓 Lunch, dinner; closed Sat lunch and Sun 🚌 23, 27, 35, 41, 42, 45

### DUCK'S AT LE MARCHÉ NOIR (££)

As its name suggests, ducks decorate this cozy restaurant that has soft candlelight and an elegantly restrained ambience. The menu delivers creative combinations of Scottish produce with an international influence. Attentive service.
➕ E6 ✉ 2/4 Eyre Place EH3 5EP ☎ 0131 558 1608 🕓 Lunch, dinner; closed lunch Sat–Mon 🚌 23, 27, 36

### GRAIN STORE (£££)

This smart restaurant has a unique setting in an 18th-century stone vaulted storeroom with archways and intimate alcoves. The well-balanced menu includes such delights as saddle of venison with chestnuts and rosemary. Very tempting home-made desserts.
➕ F9 ✉ 30 Victoria Street (1st floor) EH1 2JW ☎ 0131 225 7635 🕓 Lunch, dinner 🚌 23, 27, 41, 42, 45

### HALDANES (£££)

You will be hard pushed to find refined Scottish country house cooking to beat this. Dishes such as west coast king scallops, along with Highland venison and Scottish beef are served in the basement dining rooms, furnished with a dash of tartan. Coffee is served with home-made truffles and fudge.
➕ F7 ✉ Albany Hotel, Albany Street EH1 3QY ☎ 0131 556 8407 🕓 Dinner; lunch by reservation 🚌 8, 17

### HOWIES (£)

In a delightful 200-year-old Georgian building, this chain restaurant offers fresh Scottish produce served with imagination at a good price, and with friendly service. There are other branches in the city at Stockbridge, Victoria and Bruntsfield.
➕ F8 ✉ 29 Waterloo Place EH1 3BQ ☎ 0131 556 5766 🕓 Lunch, dinner 🚌 8, 29, 37, 37a,

### KEEPERS (££)

Intimate cellar restaurant with stone walls and flagstone floors spread over three rooms. Mainly Scottish cuisine with French overtones and good vegetarian options. If you really want to eat as the Scots do, the haggis with horseradish and Drambuie sauce should not be missed.

🖪 E7  ✉ 13b Dundas Street EH3 6QG  ☎ 0131 556 5707 Tue–Fri lunch, dinner, Sat dinner only; Sun, Mon by arrangement 🚌 23, 27

### REFORM (££)

Innovative restaurant where chef Paul Mattison's intrinsically modern menu has a strong Scottish theme dashed with intense, inspired tastes. Interesting wine list.

🖪 G9  ✉ 267 Canongate, Royal Mile EH8 8BQ  ☎ 0131 558 9992  ◷ Lunch, dinner 🚌 35

### ROXBURGHE HOTEL (££)

Exciting creations such as loin of lamb with garlic and olive oil mash, honey-glazed veg and beetroot sweet and sour jus are served alongside traditional Scottish dishes, in an elegant Victorian dining room.

🖪 C8  ✉ 38 Charlotte Square EH2 4HQ  ☎ 0131 240 5500 ◷ Lunch, dinner; closed Sat and Sun lunch 🚌 13, 19, 36, 37, 37A, 41

### STAC POLLY (££)

Cream parchment walls, low-ceilings, red carpet and tartan-clad chairs help create an intimate atmosphere. Mostly modern Scottish cuisine with such tempting delights as baked supreme of Scottish salmon served with braised leeks, bacon dumplings and a lemon

butter sauce. Don't pass on dessert.

🖪 D9  ✉ 8–10 Grindlay Street EH3 9AS  ☎ 0131 229 5405 ◷ Lunch, dinner; closed Sat lunch and Sun 🚌 10, 11, 15/15A, 16, 17

### TOWER RESTAURANT AND TERRACE (££)

On the fifth floor of the Museum of Scotland with great views of the castle, this chic and stylish restaurant offers an interesting selection of eclectic dishes using quality Scottish ingredients.

🖪 F9  ✉ Museum of Scotland, Chambers Street EH1 1JF ☎ 0131 225 3003  ◷ Lunch, dinner 🚌 23, 27, 41, 42, 45

### WEE WINDAES (££)

Gaze out over the cobbled streets of Edinburgh's Royal Mile while tucking into fine Scottish fare by candlelight. Haggis, salmon, pheasant, Angus beef and other traditional dishes all cooked to perfection.

🖪 F9  ✉ 144 High Street EH1 1QS  ☎ 0800 698 1455 ◷ Lunch, dinner 🚌 23, 27, 35, 41

### WITCHERY BY THE CASTLE (£££)

This enchanting candle-lit restaurant is *the* place for a special night out. The cooking displays a contemporary spin on Scottish classics like game, fish and shellfish, complemented by a huge selection of wines.

🖪 E9  ✉ Castlehill, Royal Mile EH1 2NF  ☎ 0131 225 5613 Lunch, dinner 🚌 23, 27, 41, 42, 45

### WHAT'S ON THE MENU

**Arbroath smokies**—small hot-smoked haddock

**Atholl brose**—drink prepared from oatmeal and water, with whisky and honey

**black bun**—tea-time treat made from dried fruits and spices, cooked within a pastry case

**clapshot**—cooked swede and potato (neeps and tatties), mashed up with butter and milk

**clootie dumpling**—steamed sweet and spicy pudding, traditionally cooked in a cloth

**cranachan**—dessert of raspberries, cream and toasted oatmeal

**crowdie**—light curd cheese

**Cullen skink**—creamy fish broth based on 'Finnan haddie' or smoked haddock

**Forfar bridie**—meat pasty made with beef, onion and potato

**hot toddy**—warming drink made with boiling water, a little sugar and whisky, with lemon, nutmeg and cinnamon

**kedgeree**—mildy curried dish of smoked haddock with hard boiled eggs, onion and rice

**partan bree**—crab soup

**potato scone**—hot, flat, savoury cake made from potato and flour

# Fine Dining

## DINE WITH A VIEW

For fine food and spectacular views try the Forth Floor Restaurant at Harvey Nichols (✉ 33–34 St. Andrew Square EH2 2AD ☎ 0131 524 8350), which has a balcony and floor-to-ceiling windows providing striking views of the Castle in one direction and the Firth of Forth in the other. Oloroso (► 71) occupies a top-floor corner site with two sides of the building made entirely of glass and an outdoor roof terrace, which makes for stunning views of the castle and views across the roof tops to the Firth of Forth. Tower Restaurant (► 65) occupies a space above the Museum of Scotland (► 39) and offers superb views over Old Town.

## THE GRILL ROOM (£££)

The formal Grill Room focuses on traditional French cuisine with Scottish overtones in its unpretentious classic dishes. Stark white tablecloths, sparkling silver, glistening crystal, fine bone china and an intimate atmosphere set the tone for exquisite fine dining.

✚ D9 ✉ Sheraton Grand Hotel, 1 Festival Square EH3 9SR ☎ 0131 221 6422 🕐 Lunch, dinner; closed Sun, lunch Sat 🚍 1, 10, 11, 16, 34

## NUMBER ONE (£££)

Chef Jeff Bland serves luxurious simple dishes created from top-quality ingredients at this very classy restaurant. The menu has a range of meats and seafood (braised oxtail, Barbary duck, organic salmon). For dessert, the hot banana and chocolate chip soufflé is to die for.

✚ F8 ✉ Balmoral Hotel, 1 Princes Street EH2 2EQ ☎ 0131 557 6727 🕐 Lunch, dinner; closed lunch Sat 🚍 3, 10, 17 25, 44

## OFF THE WALL (£££)

An uncomplicated modern approach to cuisine leaves the perfectly prepared food to speak for itself—with the odd surprise, such as squab pigeon with black pudding and orange sauce. The setting is simple—crisp white cloths and cheerful yellow walls.

✚ F9 ✉ 105 High Street, Royal Mile EH1 1SG ☎ 0131 558 1497 🕐 Lunch, dinner; closed Sun 🚍 23, 27

## RESTAURANT AT THE BONHAM (£££)

In a boutique hotel (► 86), long windows, wooden floors and chic brown and cream livery set the perfect scene for stylish contemporary cooking. Desserts such as orange blossom panacotta with lavender tuile are almost too attractive to eat.

✚ C8 ✉ Bonham Hotel, 35 Drumsheugh Gardens EH3 7RN ☎ 0131 623 9319 🕐 Lunch, dinner 🚍 13

## RHUBARB (£££)

This impressive dining room is under the gaze of the Dick-Cunningham family, whose ancestral portraits hang on the walls. The food more than matches the opulent setting. The cooking features the best produce from small suppliers, handled in a modern, tasty and fuss-free style. You will need to take a taxi to get here but it's worth the effort.

✚ K12 ✉ Prestonfield Hotel, Priestfield Road EH16 5UT ☎ 0131 225 1333 🕐 Lunch, dinner

## VERMILION (£££)

Intimate and distinctive, Vermilion serves simple classic dishes with a contemporary twist. Handmade glasses and decanters, waxed leather chairs and bespoke cutlery lend an air of sophistication. Eclectic wine list.

✚ F8 ✉ Scotsman Hotel, 20 North Bridge EH1 1YT ☎ 0131 556 5565 🕐 Dinner Wed–Sun 🚍 3, 5, 7, 30, 31, 33, 37

# Fish, Seafood & Vegetarian

### THE BOATHOUSE (££)

A fish lover's paradise in an old whitewashed building above the beach, with views of the Firth of Forth. The dining areas have polished pine tables and display antique curios on the walls, and outside decking enables alfresco dining in summer. The menu changes daily.

➕ Off map at A4 ✉ 19b High Street, South Queensferry EH30 9PP ☎ 0131 331 5429 🕐 Lunch, dinner 🚌 43

### DAVID BANN'S VEGETARIAN RESTAURANT (££)

David Bann ensures quality and attention to detail at his well-designed bar/restaurant, which opened in 2002. Clean, rich tones, natural wood and soft lighting set the mood for modern vegetarian cuisine.

➕ G9 ✉ 56–58 St. Mary's Street EH1 1SX ☎ 0131 556 5888 🕐 Lunch, dinner 🚌 35

### HENDERSON'S SALAD TABLE (£)

An Edinburgh legend on the vegetarian scene that prides itself on good salads, plus soups, hot dishes and puddings. Lively, cosmopolitan atmosphere, and sometimes live music.

➕ E8 ✉ 94 Hanover Street EH2 1DR ☎ 0131 225 2131 🕐 Lunch, dinner; closed Sun except during Festival 🚌 19, 23, 27, 41, 42, 45

### MUSSEL INN (££)

The freshest and tastiest shellfish, scallops and oysters are delivered fresh from the Scottish sea lochs to this bustling eatery in the heart of New Town.

➕ E8 ✉ 61–65 Rose Street EH2 2NH ☎ 0131 225 5979 🕐 Lunch, dinner 🚌 3, 12, 29, 41

### SHIP ON THE SHORE (£££)

Cozy bistro-style bar with a nautical theme. Tasty seafood options may include smoked salmon with lemon, chopped onion and capers or paupiette of sole and prawns served on braised leeks.

➕ J3 ✉ 24–26 The Shore, Leith EH6 6QN ☎ 0131 555 0409 🕐 Lunch daily, dinner Mon–Sat 🚌 16, 22, 35, 36

### SHORE BAR & RESTAURANT (££)

This informal, zesty establishment in an 18th-century building serves fresh, succulent fish in its wood-panelled dining room overlooking the Water of Leith.

➕ J3 ✉ 3 Shore, Leith EH6 6QW ☎ 0131 553 5080 🕐 Lunch, dinner 🚌 16, 22, 35, 36

### WATERFRONT (££)

Extremely pretty quayside restaurant housed in a former lock-keeper's cottage, where a wide range of fresh, well-prepared fish, meat and vegetarian dishes are served in intimate booths or the vine-clad conservatory. Extensive wine list.

➕ H3 ✉ 1c Dock Place, Leith EH6 6LU ☎ 0131 554 7427 🕐 Lunch, dinner 🚌 16, 22, 35, 36

### SCOTTISH SALMON

Scottish salmon is celebrated as being among the best in the world, but beware of the variation between wild (caught) and farmed salmon. Over recent years salmon farming has been hard hit by controversy about fish kept in overcrowded sea cages, the use of dye to colour the flesh and the presence of various chemicals and pollutants. Many salmon farmers have now changed their ways, but many restaurants still consider wild salmon superior.

# Bistros and Brasseries

## FOOD ON THE RUN

Stopping for lunch often seems a waste of time when you're up to your eyes in sightseeing, but Edinburgh has lots of quick options. There are food courts in shopping malls, while many attractions have their own restaurants and cafés. American fast-food chains have reached most corners of Scotland, so you won't have to look far to find a pizza or hamburger. The city is liberally sprinkled with very good takeout sandwich bars, and many have tables if you want to rest your weary feet. Although Edinburgh has many traditional cafés, the word 'café' is used to describe the increasing number of more stylish Continental-style establishments, which bridge the gap between pubs, restaurants and coffee bars by selling coffees, snacks, wines and meals.

## ALL BAR ONE (££)

Serving a variety of bistro-style food based on simple recipes, this financial area bolt-hole has a refectory hall theme with large wooden tables.

⊞ E8 ✉ 29–31 George Street EH2 2PA ☎ 0131 226 9971
🕐 Lunch, dinner 🚌 13, 19, 41

## BLUE BAR CAFÉ (£££)

Modern brasserie with good value and imaginative choices that incorporate many influences and tastes. If you prefer something light, try a crayfish sandwich or a bowl of white bean and chorizo soup. For a more substantial meal, there's carpaccio of beef with Parmesan cheese followed by corn-fed chicken with aromatic leek risotto and bacon dressing.

⊞ D9 ✉ 10 Cambridge Street EH1 2ED ☎ 0131 221 1222
🕐 Lunch, dinner; closed Sun
🚌 10, 11, 16, 22

## DOME (£££)

Classy venue housed in a converted bank with a magnificent glass dome as the centrepiece in the Grill Room bistro. Classic Scottish cuisine surprisingly blended with European and Far East tastes.

⊞ E8 ✉ 14 George Street EH2 2PF ☎ 0131 624 8624
🕐 Lunch, dinner 🚌 13, 19, 41

## DORIC TAVERN (££)

Built in 1710, this bustling bistro has become a meeting place for writers, artists and journalists. Eclectic dishes include fillet of venison, steaks and pastas, and sweet potato pie, plus the upbeat downstairs pub serves traditional pub snacks.

⊞ F9 ✉ 15–16 Market Street EH1 1DE ☎ 0131 225 1084
🕐 Lunch, dinner 🚌 23, 27, 41

## HADRIAN'S BRASSERIE (££)

Chic informal brasserie decorated in lime green and a dash of violet, with walnut fittings. Good quality Scottish cuisine with a European influence.

⊞ F8 ✉ Balmoral Hotel, 1 Princes Street EH2 2EQ
☎ 0131 557 5000 🕐 Lunch, dinner 🚌 3, 10, 17, 25, 44

## LE SEPT (££)

Vibrant French bistro with a light and airy feel and bright Parisian posters on the wall. Crêpes with a wide range of delicious fillings are the house special, but there are many other dishes available.

⊞ F9 ✉ 5 Hunter Square EH1 1QW ☎ 0131 225 5428
🕐 Lunch, dinner 🚌 23, 35, 41

## ROGUE (££)

A stylish yet affordable haunt enhanced by cool black furniture and crisp white tablecloths. Dishes include such delights as fillet of beef with black truffle and foie gras butter on spinach and noodles, or breast of guinea fowl with pilaff of red Camargue rice and salsa verde.

⊞ D10 ✉ 67 Morrison Street EH3 8BU ☎ 0131 228 2700
🕐 Lunch, dinner; closed Sun
🚌 2, 34, 35

# Snacks/Light Bites

**BENNETS BAR (£)**

Popular with actors from the nearby Kings Theatre, this Victorian bar prides itself on sound simple home-made food at a good price, and 100 or so malt whiskies. The elaborate interior includes stained glass, tiles, mirrors and carved wood.

➕ D11 ✉ 8 Leven Street EH3 9LG ☎ 0131 229 5143 🕐 Bar meals: Mon—Sat noon—2, 5—8.30 🚍 11, 17, 23

**CIRCUS CAFÉ (££)**

An exciting addition to the Edinburgh café scene, Circus Café is much more than a café—it's also a restaurant/bar, bakery, takeout and food hall all under one roof.

➕ D7 ✉ 15 North West Circus Place EH3 6SX ☎ 0131 220 0333 🕐 Lunch, dinner 🚍 19, 24, 29, 42

**ELEPHANT HOUSE (£)**

A popular café offering snacks, light meals and a mouth-watering array of cakes, accompanied by excellent coffees and teas.

➕ F9 ✉ 21 George 1V Bridge EH1 1EN ☎ 0131 220 5355 🕐 Lunch, dinner 🚍 23, 27, 35, 41, 42

**MONSTER MASH (££)**

Sausage and mashed potato is staging a come back here. The bangers come in many flavours, such as Auld Reekie (smoked) and Mediterranean (with basil and sun-dried tomatoes), and there is a variety of mash, too. Plastic tomato-shaped ketchup bottles add a large helping of nostalgia.

➕ F10 ✉ 40 Forrest Road EH1 2QN ☎ 0131 225 70694 🕐 Lunch, dinner 🚍 35, 45

**OLIVE BRANCH (££)**

A trendy mix of black leather, wicker and velour seating in neutral shades against wooden floors and bare brick walls. Large windows enable serious people-watching in an area that is popular for the wild and bold.

➕ F7 ✉ 91 Broughton Street EH1 3RX ☎ 0131 557 8589 🕐 Lunch, dinner 🚍 8, 17

**SPOON (£)**

Unusual sandwich fillings such as Parmesan cheese with marinated anchovies or smoked pork with apple chutney are loaded onto thick wholemeal bread, panini or focaccia. Salads and fresh fruit juices, too. Huge windows, beech tables and soothing blue hues exude a clean, minimalist feel.

➕ G9 ✉ 15 Blackfriars Street EH1 1NB ☎ 0131 556 6922 🕐 Mon—Sat 8am—6pm 🚍 23, 35, 41

**STARBANK INN (££)**

Right on the waterfront, the Starbank Inn offers traditional pub food, such as roast lamb with mint sauce, poached salmon, or chicken with tarragon cream sauce, and splendid views over the Firth of Forth.

➕ E2 ✉ 64 Laverockbank Road, Trinity EH5 3BZ ☎ 0131 552 4141 🕐 Lunch, dinner 🚍 7, 10, 11, 16

**PUB GRUB**

Central-city dining pubs traditionally serve snacks and light meals such as sandwiches, toasted sandwiches, filled potatoes and ploughmans (bread, cheese and pickles). Nowadays many have extended their menu to such dishes as curry, steak and ale pie, steak and chips or even haggis and neeps (a blend of swede and potato mashed with butter and milk). But, on the whole, pub food in Scotland is not overly imaginative. Most (but not all) pubs welcome families and many stay open throughout the day, though food is often available only from 12–2 and 6–9. A new breed of so-called gastropubs has set about catering for those who rate good food as highly as a good pint of beer.

# International Cuisine

## EXOTIC TASTES

While local dishes are still prominent in most of Scotland, in Edinburgh the choice of cuisines from around the world is endless. From Moroccan and Turkish to Thai and Indian—some restaurants offer exciting fusions of Indian and European cooking or the very latest innovations from Mumbai (Bombay). Newer international trends include Indonesian, Caribbean, Vietnamese, Hungarian, Russian, Mongolian and Mexican.

### BELUGA BAR & CANTEEN (£££)

Stained-glass windows throw vivid light across the wooden floor and dark walls, while a waterfall trickles in the background. The food is as contemporary as the interior, with a heavy slant towards Asian and Pacific Rim ingredients.
🔢 F9 ✉ 30a Chambers Street EH1 1HU ☎ 0131 624 4545 🕐 Lunch, dinner 🚌 23, 27, 41, 42

### LE CAFÉ ST. HONORÉ (££)

Intimate, relaxed dining in an authentic French-style restaurant. The menu has a fine blend of Scottish and French dishes with Continental flair. Extensive wine list.
🔢 E8 ✉ 34 NW Thistle Street Lane EH2 1EA ☎ 0131 226 2211 🕐 Lunch, dinner; closed Sun 🚌 23, 29, 41

### COSMO (££)

This old-fashioned restaurant has been a benchmark for Italian food for over 30 years. A loyal clientele return time and time again to sample quality 1960s-style Italian cooking, with wines to match. Reserve ahead.
🔢 D8 ✉ 58a North Castle Street EH2 3LU ☎ 0131 226 6743 🕐 Lunch, dinner; closed lunch Sat, Sun 🚌 19, 29, 37

### LA GARRIGUE (£££)

A showcase for food from the Languedoc region in France, the hearty Gallic cooking is presented with finesse and the wines and cheeses are also sourced from the region. Cool blue walls and wooden furniture give a Mediterranean feel.
🔢 F8 ✉ 31 Jeffrey Street EH1 1DH ☎ 0131 557 3032 🕐 Lunch, dinner 🚌 23, 35, 41

### IGGS (££)

Convivial Old Town restaurant with fine views of Calton Hill. The quality organic Scottish cuisine has a Mediterranean influence; there is a Spanish tapas bar next door. Try poached lobster on truffled leeks with lobster caviar sauce, or, for vegetarians, Spanish Gypsy vegetable stew.
🔢 F8 ✉ 15 Jeffrey Street EH1 1DR ☎ 0131 557 8184 🕐 Lunch, dinner; closed Sun 🚌 30, 35

### KWEILIN (££)

Enjoy beautifully cooked traditional Cantonese cuisine in plush surroundings. The menu offers a great selection and there is an excellent wine list.
🔢 E7 ✉ 19–21 Dundas Street EH3 6QQ ☎ 0131 557 1875 🕐 Lunch, dinner; closed Mon 🚌 23, 27

### MARTINS RESTAURANT (£££)

Attentive staff serve modern European food cooked with precision at this quiet restaurant. Lamb stuffed with spinach and truffle mousse is accompanied by an aubergine and ratatouille timbale, while sea bream is served with sun-dried tomato couscous, baby fennel and roast butternut squash. Reservations are advisable.

🕂 E8 ✉ 70 Rose Street, North Lane EH2 3DX ☎ 0131 225 3106 🕐 Lunch, dinner; closed Sun, Mon 🚌 23, 29, 41

### OLOROSO (£££)

An architectural gem, with floor-to-ceiling glass walls offering panoramic views. Innovative dishes have an Asian influence, such as seared sea bass with butternut squash purée, and chicory and white bean sauce. Have a drink on the terrace for a great view of the castle.

🕂 D8 ✉ 33 Castle Street EH2 3DN ☎ 0131 226 7614 🕐 Lunch, dinner 🚌 19, 37, 41

### PANCHO VILLAS (££)

Mexican-born owner, Mayra Nunez has brought a taste of home to Edinburgh through her authentic home-made dishes served in an informal, lively atmosphere.

🕂 G9 ✉ 240 Canongate EH9 8AB ☎ 0131 557 4416 🕐 Lunch, dinner; closed lunch Sun 🚌 35

### LA P'TITE FOLIE 2 (££)

The French cuisine more than measures up to the outstanding Tudor building housing this cheerful eatery where the tables are close together but no one seems to care. French staff cater to your every need.

🕂 C8 ✉ Tudor House, 9 Randolph Place EH3 7TE ☎ 0131 225 8678 🕐 Lunch, dinner 🚌 13, 19, 36. 37, 41

### RESTAURANT MARTIN WISHART (£££)

Michelin-starred Martin Wishart's brilliantly executed dishes are beautifully presented at this tiny French restaurant on the waterfront at Leith. Bright, modern art stands out against the white walls and stone floors.

🕂 J3 ✉ 54 The Shore, Leith EH6 6RA ☎ 0131 553 3557 🕐 Lunch, dinner; closed Sun, Mon, lunch Sat 🚌 16, 22, 35, 36

### SANTINI (££–£££)

This elegant venue includes Santini Bis, an informal all-day option offering pizza, pasta and lighter dishes. The main restaurant is decorated in neutral shades with lots of glass and chrome and offers outstanding Italian dishes such as creamy porcini mushroom risotto.

🕂 D9 ✉ 8 Conference Square EH3 8AN ☎ 0131 221 7788 🕐 Lunch, dinner; closed Sun, lunch Sat 🚌 22, 30

### VINCAFFE (££)

The owners of Scotland's oldest delicatessen, Valvona and Crolla (► 74), opened this café/wine bar in 2004, creating a Continental-style meeting place. Their own finest ingredients are used to provide simple or sophisticated Italian food, washed down by a glass of wine from their range.

🕂 F8 ✉ 11 Multrees Walk EH1 3DQ ☎ 0131 557 0088 🕐 Lunch, dinner; closed dinner Sun 🚌 8, 12, 10, 11, 16

### EATING ITALIAN

Large numbers of Italians emigrated to Scotland in the early 20th century, bringing with them their own culinary influences. Hence, you will find many good Italian restaurants, mostly in Edinburgh's West End. The following are just a few of the best:

**Bar Napoli** (✉ 75 Hanover Street EH2 1EE ☎ 0131 225 2600) is a long-standing popular choice that offers good Neapolitan cuisine.

**Est Est Est** (✉ 135 George Street EH2 4JS ☎ 0131 225 2555) has a buzzy light and airy atmosphere that always pulls in a crowd, and rightly so.

**Bellini** (✉ 8b Abercromby Place, off Queen Street EH3 6LB ☎ 0131 476 2602) has Italian chef Angelo Cimini, who prepares secret recipes, hundreds of years old, that are served in an elegant Georgian dining room.

**Bar Roma** (✉ 39a Queensferry Street EH2 4RA ☎ 0131 226 2977), established over 22 years ago, is a vibrant family restaurant with a Continental feel.

# Woollens, Tartan & Clothing

## SCOTTISH WOOL

If you're looking for the very best in Scottish woollen items, you could spend a small fortune on designer cashmere in Edinburgh, but equally, you'll find a plethora of factory outlets with good quality knitwear at knock-down prices, particularly cashmere. However, you are unlikely to find anything leading the way in designer fashion at the mill outlets. Serious knitters will delight in the huge range of yarns available in every conceivable shade, at a good price.

## ARMSTRONGS

Established in 1840, museum-like Armstrong's is well-known for its unusual shop, Scotland's largest emporium of sassy, retro and traditional Scottish clothing. There is another branch at Clerk Street.

✚ D9 ✉ 83 Grassmarket EH1 2HJ ☎ 0131 220 5557 🚌 2

## BELINDA ROBERTSON

Scotland's renowned cashmere designer has come to the heart of Edinburgh's New Town. Belinda's creations, which include sweaters, gloves and scarves as well as cashmere knickers and G-strings, have been donned by the likes of Nicole Kidman and Madonna.

✚ E7 ✉ 13 Dundas Street EH3 6QG ☎ 0131 225 057 🚌 19, 23, 27

## THE CASHMERE STORE

Come to this Royal Mile store for a touch of luxury. Anything you could want in cashmere is here—sweaters, cardigans, scarves, dresses and skirts.

✚ F9 ✉ 379 High Street EH1 1PT ☎ 0131 225 5178 🚌 35 and all North Bridge buses

## DESIGNS ON CASHMERE

Pamper yourself with one of these exquisite Scottish cashmere garments, for men and women. Beware, quality comes at a price.

✚ G9 ✉ 28 High Street EH1 1TB ☎ 0131 556 6394 🚌 3, 30, 31, 32, 35, 37, 49

## DICKSON & MACNAUGHTON

For the archetypal country gentleman (or woman), this established store creates authentic surroundings to sell high-quality country clothing by all the leading manufacturers. They also stock a full range of fishing and shooting accessories.

✚ E8 ✉ 21 Frederick Street EH2 2NE ☎ 0131 225 4218 🚌 19, 29, 41

## FRONTIERS

One of many woollen shops on the Royal Mile. The high quality is reflected in the prices. Handmade knitwear, including stylish cashmere and woollen accessories, sweaters, bags and scarves.

✚ G9 ✉ 254 Canongate EH8 8AA ☎ 0131 556 2791 🚌 35

## GEOFFREY (TAILOR) KILTMAKERS

Specialists in traditional, casual and modern kilt-making, and outfitters for men, women and children.

✚ G9 ✉ 57–59 High Street EH1 1SR ☎ 0131 557 0256 🚌 23, 27, 35

## HAWICK CASHMERE COMPANY

Cashmere doesn't come cheap and the bottom line for a sweater from this shop is £100—the 'Cashmere Made In Scotland' label attached to each garment satisfies that the clothes are of the highest quality. Also sweaters and scarves in every shade.

➕ E9 ✉ 71–81 Grassmarket EH1 2HJ ☎ 0131 225 8634 🚌 2

## HECTOR RUSSELL

Part of a well-known chain of kilt shops, this branch allows you to rent, as well as buy. It's all here, from a *sgian dubh* (small knife worn inside the sock) to the complete outfit. The shop will arrange for your purchases to be mailed home. Additional branches are in High Street and Lawnmarket.
➕ E8 ✉ 95 Princes Street EH2 2ER ☎ 0131 225 3315; freephone order number (UK only) 0800 980 4010 🚌 3, 10, 17, 25, 44

## JANE DAVIDSON

Owner Sarah Davidson has built her reputation on providing excellent service. The three-floor Georgian town house stocks exclusive cashmere labels from around the world including N. Peal and Anne Storey.
➕ E8 ✉ 52 Thistle Street EH2 1EN ☎ 0131 225 3280 🚌 23, 29, 41

## KINLOCH ANDERSON

While browsing for tartan trousers, jackets, kilt outfits, skirts and accessories, you can learn more about the history of tartan from the exhibition displayed at this Leith establishment, experts in kilts, tartans and Highland dress since 1868.
➕ H3 ✉ Commercial Street/Dock Street, Leith EH6 6EY ☎ 0131 555 1390 🚌 16, 22, 25, 36

## LINZI CRAWFORD

Sole stockist of several emerging European labels, along with Linzi's own line of merino and cashmere in a variety of distinct shades.
➕ F7 ✉ 27 Dublin Street EH3 6NL ☎ 0131 558 7558 🚌 13

## RAGAMUFFIN

Displays of vivid handmade chunky knitwear, scarves and toys from all over England and Scotland catch your eye in the huge windows of this shop on the corner of St. Mary's Street.
➕ G9 ✉ 276 Canongate EH8 8AA ☎ 0131 557 6007 🚌 35

## STEWART CHRISTIE & CO.

Bespoke tailors for more than 200 years, making garments on the premises. This family business provides a range of country and formal clothing, including Scottish tweed jackets and moleskin trousers as well as Highland dress and tartan evening trousers.
➕ D8 ✉ 63 Queen Street EH2 4NA ☎ 0131 225 6639 🚌 12, 13, 15, 23, 27, 29, 42

## TISO

Helpful staff offer knowledgeable advice on the quality outdoor clothing and equipment they sell here—all you need for walking, climbing, camping or skiing, and there is also a good mountaineering and travel book section.
➕ D8 ✉ 123–125 Rose Street EH2 3DT ☎ 0131 225 9486 🚌 23, 29, 41

## DESIGNER FASHION

Until not so long ago, Glasgow was considered to rule supreme over Edinburgh when it came to shopping for designer names. But now things have changed. Edinburgh is challenging its rival with stylish home-grown boutiques, international fashion outlets and top department stores. A string of designer names have extended their empires to Edinburgh, including Emporio Armani (✉ 25 Multrees Walk EH1 3DQ ☎ 0131 523 1580); Louis Vuitton (✉ 1–2 Multrees Walk EH1 3DQ ☎ 020 7399 4050); Hugo Boss (✉ 94 George Street EH2 3DF ☎ 0131 226 3524); Karen Millen (✉ 53 George Street EH2 2HT ☎ 0131 220 1589); Hobbs (✉ 47 George Street EH2 2HT ☎ 020 220 5386), with other big names in the pipeline.

# Food & Drink

## HAGGIS

Haggis is Scotland's national dish and comes from an ancient recipe for using up the cheapest cuts of meat. It's a sort of large mutton sausage based on the ground-up liver, lungs and heart of a sheep, mixed with oatmeal, onion and spices, and cooked up in the sheep's stomach. It can be dry, greasy or gritty, although when made properly can be delicious—a wee dram of whisky helps wash it down. These days restaurants serve their own spicy versions of the recipe, and if you want a small taster, you'll sometimes find it on the menu as a starter.

## AU GOURMAND

Sample the tastes and aromas of provincial France at this little shop, where the smell of freshly cooked bread is irresistible.

⊞ E6 ✉ 1 Brandon Terrace EH3 5EA ☎ 0131 624 4666 🚌 8, 13, 17

## BAXTERS

A large food hall generated from the famous Scottish family selling all Baxter products, and lots more.

⊞ H2 ✉ Ocean Terminal, Leith EH6 6JG ☎ 0131 553 0840 🚌 1, 11, 22, 34, 35, 36

## DEMIJOHN

A liquid deli where you are encouraged to taste the products and personalize them with your choice of bottle; liqueurs, spirits, whisky, oils, vinegars and spices from around the world.

⊞ F9 ✉ 32 Victoria Street EH1 2JW ☎ 0131 225 3265 🚌 2, 23, 27, 35, 41

## IAN MELLIS

Lovers of cheese owe it to themselves to visit this cheesemonger, where taste comes first. The range of Scottish cheeses is overwhelming, but staff will help find the perfect cheese for your palate.

⊞ F9 ✉ 30a Victoria Street EH1 2JW ☎ 0131 226 6215 🚌 2, 23, 27, 35, 41

## MAXWELL & KENNEDY

A tempting display of handmade Belgian chocolates and truffles presented in beautiful boxes.

⊞ F8 ✉ 3 Waverley Bridge EH1 1BQ ☎ 0131 558 1619 🚌 3, 10, 17, 23, 24, 27, 44

## PECKHAMS

Discover the famed MacSween's award-winning haggis, deemed to be the best in Scotland, along with an array of other Scottish specialties.

⊞ D12 ✉ 155–159 Bruntsfield Place EH10 4DG ☎ 0131 229 7054 🚌 11, 15, 16, 17, 23

## ROYAL MILE WHISKIES

Enthusiasts are on hand to offer advice on the hundreds of single malt whiskies stocked here—some are 100 years old and some are rare. Have your items shipped home, or order by phone or online (www. royalmilewhiskies.com).

⊞ F9 ✉ 379 High Street EH1 1PW ☎ 0131 225 3383 🚌 23, 27, 35, 41, 42

## VALVONA AND CROLLA

Much-loved deli that has hardly changed since opening in 1934. Ceiling-high shelves are stacked with the finest Italian produce and wines: mozzarella is shipped from Naples; an array of cured meats hang from the ceiling; and bread is baked daily.

⊞ G7 ✉ 19 Elm Row EH7 4AA ☎ 0131 556 6066 🚌 7, 10, 14, 16, 31

## WILLIAM CADENHEAD

A quaint shop hidden at the bottom of the Royal Mile, specializing in malt whiskies and old oak-matured Demerara rum.

⊞ G8 ✉ 172 Canongate EH8 8BN ☎ 0131 556 5864 🚌 35

# Jewellery & Accessories

### CARINA SHOES
Superb Continental leather footwear for ladies from the likes of Renata, Gine, Magrit, Rebeca Sanver, Paco Herrero, Pertti Palmroth, and matching handbags and accessories.

➕ F8  ✉ 25–27 Jeffrey Street EH1 1DH  ☎ 0131 558 3344
🚌 23, 35, 41

### HAMILTON & INCHES
Established in 1866, the city's most reputable jeweller offers fine imaginative jewellery and silverware. In a grand old building with workshops above and an ornate interior complete with chandeliers.

➕ E8  ✉ 87 George Street EH2 2EY  ☎ 0131 225 4898
🚌 13, 19, 37, 41

### HELEN BATEMAN
For bona fide one-offs designed by the owner, visit this exclusive store that displays a superb range of shoes, boots and accessories that will appeal to most tastes.

➕ C9  ✉ 16 William Street EH3 7NH  ☎ 0131 220 4495
🚌 4, 12, 25

### JOSEPH BONNAR
In business since the 1960s, Joseph Bonnar boasts Scotland's largest range of antique jewellery, plus other items made of precious metals.

➕ E8  ✉ 72 Thistle Street EH2 1EN  ☎ 0131 226 2811
🚌 23, 27, 29

### MACKENZIE LEATHER GOODS
Wonderfully crafted leather bags, suitcases and other items of a very high quality.

➕ F9  ✉ 34 Victoria Street EH1 2JW  ☎ 0131 220 0089
🚌 2, 23, 27, 35, 41

### ORTAK
Leading gold and silver jewellery manufacturer with a range of classic jewellery and gifts in delicate, innovative designs, hand-finished to the highest standards. Based on techniques unique to the Orkney Islands, handed down over the decades.

➕ F8  ✉ Princess Mall, Princes Street EH1 1BQ  ☎ 0131 557 4393  🚌 23, 27, 41, 42, 100

### PALENQUE
Palenque specializes in competitively priced contemporary and silver rings, necklaces and bracelets and hand-crafted accessories.

➕ G9  ✉ 56 High Street EH1 1TB  ☎ 0131 557 9553
🚌 35 and all North Bridge buses

### SCOTTISH GEMS
A distinctive blue façade conceals an outstanding selection of Scottish-made silver and gold jewellery—some handmade.

➕ G9  ✉ 24 High Street EH1 1TB  ☎ 0131 557 5731
🚌 35 and all North Bridge buses

### THE TAPPIT HEN
This tiny shop specializes in traditional Celtic knotwork wedding rings, handmade in precious metals, plus a range of gifts made from pewter.

➕ F8  ✉ 89 High Street EH1 1SG  ☎ 0131 557 1852  🚌 35 and all North Bridge buses

### WILLIAM STREET
This cobbled street in Edinburgh's West End (at the junction of Stafford and Alva streets) has a concentration of small, specialized shops. Many independent designers have set up shop, selling exclusive clothes, accessories and gifts, such as Helen Bateman (➤ this page), Fling (➤ 78) and Arkangel (No. 4 ☎ 0131 225 9602). Master milliner Yvette Jelfs at No. 35 (☎ 0131 225 6969) sells exquisite hand-finished hats, bags and scarves, in unique designs and personalized to customers' requirements. William Street attracts women who want to indulge and pamper themselves, while their men rest their legs in one of the old traditional pubs, which help to retain the original character of the street. Hairdresser Brian Rafferty has a shop here. He styles the Queen's hair when she is in residence at Holyrood House and his shop has 'by Royal appointment' status.

# Books & Music

## BAGPIPES

The bagpipes are synonymous with Scotland. You see them everywhere, from the Military Tattoo in Edinburgh to school sports days and agricultural shows. There are many types played in a variety of countries throughout the world, and, surprisingly, the bagpipes' origins are not Scottish but possibly from ancient Egypt or Greece. A simple pipe was probably used in Scotland from medieval times but the highly developed Scottish Highland bagpipe was first used in the 16th century, mainly for signalling and to spur the troops on in battle. Each Highland regiment of the British army had its own pipers and pipebands.

## ANALOGUE

A bookshop with a difference that stocks design and contemporary culture books, and also a selection of magazines, music, posters and T-shirts.
✚ F9  ✉ 102 West Bow EH1 2HH  ☎ 0131 220 0601
🚌 2, 23, 27, 35, 41

## BAGPIPES GALORE

Listen before you buy at this atmospheric shop selling Scottish-made bagpipes for beginners or the more proficient. Pipe books, CDs and accessories, too.
✚ G9  ✉ 82 Canongate EH8 8BZ  ☎ 07000 474737  🚌 35

## BLACKFRIARS MUSIC

You can consult with the knowledgeable staff or pick up a magazine to broaden your horizons before making your choice from the good range of folk and traditional Scottish music and instruments.
✚ G9  ✉ 49 Blackfriars Street EH1 1NB  ☎ 0131 557 3090
🚌 23, 35, 41

## BLACKWELLS

This large company, with several branches throughout Edinburgh, has been providing a comprehensive range of general and academic books and publications for more than 150 years.
✚ G9  ✉ 53–62 South Bridge Street EH1 1YS  ☎ 0131 622 8222  🚌 3, 5, 7, 14, 29, 30, 31, 33, 37, 49

## FOPP

CDs and vinyls spanning every music genre, books, films and DVDs all at very competitive prices. Have a drink from the bar while browsing.
✚ F8  ✉ 7 Rose Street EH2 2PR  ☎ 0131 220 0310
🚌 23, 27, 41

## MCNAUGHTAN'S BOOKSHOP

A highly respected second-hand and antiquarian bookshop where casual browsing can sometimes unearth a real gem. The helpful owner, Elizabeth Strong, will search for specific titles.
✚ G7  ✉ 3a/4a Haddington Place, Leith Walk EH7 4AE
☎ 0131 556 5897  🚌 7, 10, 11, 12, 14, 16, 22, 25, 34, 49

## OLD TOWN BOOKSHOP

Second-hand books on Scotland and Scottish writers, plus poetry, music, travel, art and lots more. Also has a wide selection of prints and maps.
✚ F9  ✉ 8 Victoria Street EH1 2HG  ☎ 0131 225 9237
🚌 2, 23, 27, 35, 41

## WATERSTONE'S

Edinburgh has several branches of this leading bookshop. The one at the west end of Princes Street spreads over several floors, with large windows and a café on the top level that gives great views to the castle. More branches are at the east end of Princes Street, as well as George Street and Ocean Terminal.
✚ D8  ✉ 128 Princes Street EH2 4AD  ☎ 0131 226 2666
🚌 3, 10, 17, 23, 24, 27, 44 & others

# Department Stores & Shopping Malls

### FRASERS

This popular department store offers a comprehensive selection of clothes (including designer names like DKNY and Ralph Lauren), accessories, perfumes and kitchenware. There is a café on the fifth floor.

✚ D9 ✉ 145 Princes Street EH2 4YZ ☎ 0131 225 2472; www.houseoffraser.co.uk 🚍 3, 10, 17, 23, 24, 27, 44 & others

### HARVEY NICHOLS

Scotland's first branch of this exclusive London department store added a touch of glamour when it opened in Edinburgh in 2002. Perfumes, designer handbags, accessories and clothes including Gucci, Burberry, Prada, Fendi and Dior. A bar, brasserie and top-floor restaurant add plenty of options for refreshment.

✚ F8 ✉ 30–34 St. Andrew Square EH2 3AD ☎ 0131 524 8388; www.harveynichols.com 🚍 8, 10, 11, 12, 16

### JENNERS

Edinburgh's grand old dame was founded in 1838 and occupies a magnificent building. The rabbit warren inside, with a central galleried arcade, houses over 100 departments, from clothes and shoes to perfume, glassware, groceries and toys. There are four cafés.

✚ E8 ✉ 48 Princes Street Edinburgh EH2 2YJ ☎ 0131 225 2442; www.jenners.com 🚍 3, 10, 17, 23, 24, 27, 44 & others

### OCEAN TERMINAL SHOPPING CENTRE

Overlooking the Firth of Forth, this glass-and-steel retail oasis was designed by Jasper Conran and opened in 2001. The complex comes complete with high street names such as Debenhams, Dorothy Perkins, French Connection and Body Shop, plus a cinema. The central tent-like space is a venue for exhibitions. Huge free parking area.

✚ H2 ✉ Ocean Drive, Leith EH6 6JJ ☎ 0131 555 8888; www.oceanterminal.com 🚍 1, 11, 22, 34, 35, 36

### PRINCES MALL

Light and spacious shopping mall with more than 50 stores, including popular high street outlets and specialty shops. There is a rooftop café and a food court in the lower mall. Next to Waverley train station.

✚ F8 ✉ Princes Street EH1 1BQ ☎ 0131 557 3759; www.princesmall-edinburgh.co.uk 🚍 23, 27, 41, 42, 100

### ST. JAMES CENTRE

Modern shopping mall at the east end of Princes Street. Apart from more than 50 of the usual high street names, the main draw here is the John Lewis department store, which has the largest choice of goods under one roof and a café with panoramic views.

✚ F8 ✉ Leith Street EH1 3SS ☎ 0131 557 0050; www.thestjames.co.uk 🚍 1, 5, 7, 14, 19, 22, 25, 34

### WALK THE WALK

Multrees Walk–or The Walk as its known–has provided a new focal point for designer shopping in Edinburgh, creating a stylish pedestrianized shopping street anchored at one corner by the five-floor Harvey Nichols department store. The Walk has attracted a whole host of prestigious international retailers to the street, such as Links of London, Bagatt, Azendi, Calvin Klein, Louis Vuitton, Emporio Armani, with still more to come. The south end of the street leads out onto St. Andrews Square, one of the most prestigious addresses in the city.

### LEITH MARKET

The permanent covered market at Leith was first set up in March 2005 and offers a high quality mix of food, fashion, crafts, antiques, furniture, books and music. It operates every weekend, Saturday (🕐 9–5.30) and Sunday (🕐 10–4) and is situated at Leith's Commercial Quay (🚍 16, 22, 35, 36).

# Gifts & Souvenirs

## MORE GIFT IDEAS

There are two things that many visitors take home as a souvenir from Edinburgh, a bottle of malt whisky and something tartan. There are other keep-sakes that might catch your eye. Check out museum and art gallery shops, which sell items not found in other retail outlets.

Established in 1867, Edinburgh Crystal has continued to develop the art of glass-making brought to the city by the Venetians in the 17th century, and available in a range of formats from delicate glasses to dazzling paperweights. At the Edinburgh Crystal Visitor Centre (☎ 01968 675128) in Penicuik (16km/10 miles south) you can see how the glass is made and browse the shop, which stocks a full range of products.

### ANTA

Stylish shop selling Highland-made and designed fabrics, throws and cushions in wool and tweed in a range of trendy and classic tartans. Also stoneware, tiles and luggage.
✚ G9 ✉ 32 High Street, Royal Mile EH1 1TB ☎ 0131 557 8300 🚌 35 and all North Bridge buses

### CIGAR BOX

Every conceivable cigar can be found at this Royal Mile retailer that has achieved the Gold Standard in Habanos. From famous names like Montecristo and Romeo y Julieta to cigars from as far afield as Honduras, Nicaragua, and beyond.
✚ F9 ✉ 361 High Street EH1 1PW ☎ 0131 225 3534 🚌 35 and all North Bridge buses

### EDINBURGH BEAR COMPANY

Charming shop crammed with teddy bears from around the world. Paddington and Pooh and every bear in between are all here, plus limited editions and many hand-made in Scotland.
✚ G9 ✉ 46 High Street EH1 1TB ☎ 0131 557 9564 🚌 35 and all North Bridge buses

### FLING

Fresh and modern shop using cashmere, leather, and silk to produce a range of luxury gifts and accessories. Many items have been designed by owner Deirdre Nicholls.
✚ C9 ✉ 18 William Street EH3 7NH ☎ 0131 226 4114 🚌 4, 12, 25

### HALIBUT & HERRING

For a gift with a difference head to this small shop. Heavenly smells and vibrant hues tempt you to browse the huge selection of bathtime products, such as handmade soaps, bath bombs and washbags.
✚ F9 ✉ 89 West Bow EH1 2JP ☎ 0131 226 7472 🚌 2, 23, 27, 35, 41

### STUDIO ONE

West End shop in a basement setting, popular for fun and funky gifts, furnishings and household items.
✚ C9 ✉ 10–16 Stafford Street EH3 7AU ☎ 0131 226 5812 🚌 12, 25, 44

### MR WOOD'S FOSSILS

A unique shop selling, and still unearthing, fossils of all types, both plants and animals. Founded in 1983, it first supplied museums but now specializes in retailing fossils, crystals and minerals from Scotland and all over the world. Knowledgeable and friendly staff will fill you in on Lizzie, the oldest reptile ever discovered.
✚ E9 ✉ 5 Cowgatehead EH1 1JY ☎ 0131 220 1344 🚌 2, 23, 28, 41, 45

### YE OLDE CHRISTMAS SHOPPE

This family-run shop sets a festive scene with its Christmassy red façade, warm atmosphere and its hand-crafted festive mementos.
✚ G8 ✉ 145 Canongate EH8 8BN ☎ 0131 557 9220 🚌 35

# Art, Antiques & Collectables

### ADAM ANTIQUES

Large showroom of 18th- and 19th-century furniture—chests, chairs, tables, wardrobes. Restoration work is undertaken.

✚ E7 ✉ 23c Dundas Street EH3 6QQ ☎ 0131 556 7555 🚍 19, 23, 27

### AMBER ANTIQUES

Housed in a room of Gladstone's Land (► 54) with an original 17th-century painted ceiling. Mostly small curios of silver, porcelain, and glass. Also jewellery.

✚ F9 ✉ 483 Lawnmarket EH6 4PY ☎ 0794 776 4691 🚍 2, 23, 27, 35, 41, 42

### ANTHONY WOODD GALLERY

Traditional art—mainly 19th century oils, watercolours and prints, from landscapes to caricatures and sporting and military subjects. Also excellent contemporary art.

✚ E7 ✉ 4 Dundas Street EH3 6HZ ☎ 0131 558 9544 🚍 19, 23, 27

### ART ET FACTS

Huge selection of prints and originals by top British artists, such as Jack Vettriano, James McIntosh Patrick, Lynn Hanley and Simon Bull.

✚ C7 ✉ 19 Roseburn Terrace EH12 5NG ☎ 0131 346 7730 🚍 12, 26, 31

### BOW WELL

Small shop crammed with all things Scottish, including the odd antler; jewellery, weapons, Highland dress, clocks, silver, paintings, ceramics and glass, plus unusual medical and scientific equipment.

✚ F9 ✉ 103–105 West Bow EH1 2JP ☎ 0131 225 3335 🚍 2, 23, 27, 41

### BYZANTIUM

Go through an arched doorway to discover 15 stalls, spread over two floors, bursting with antiques, books, prints and lots more, where you can unearth a treasure or just browse for the fun of it.

✚ F9 ✉ 9 Victoria Street EH1 2HE ☎ No phone 🚍 2, 23, 27, 35, 41

### CARSON CLARK

Wonderful gallery specializing in antique maps and sea charts from all over the globe, dating from the 16th to 19th centuries.

✚ G8 ✉ 181–183 Canongate EH8 8BN ☎ 0131 556 4710 🚍 35

### DUNDAS STREET GALLERY

Rented by different exhibitors for short displays, this is a good-sized space for viewing mainly Scottish contemporary art.

✚ E7 ✉ 6a Dundas Street EH3 6HZ ☎ 0131 558 9363 🚍 19, 23, 27

### RANDOLPH GALLERY

Small space with changing exhibitions dealing mainly in realist art from local artists. Dundas Street is the city's main street for contemporary art.

✚ E7 ✉ 39 Dundas Street EH3 6QQ ☎ 0131 556 0808 🚍 19, 23, 27

### HIDDEN GEMS

For those on the antiques trail, some of Edinburgh's best-kept secrets are hidden away in the many tiny streets parallel with the New Town thoroughfares. Grassmarket has a wealth of antiques and curio shops, as well as collectables, second-hand clothes and books. Hopeful bargain hunters flock here to find that rare Scottish book, an ancient claymore or perhaps some 1960s ephemera. Victoria Street is an atmospheric curling, cobbled lane running from the Royal Mile down towards the Grassmarket–an ideal spot to uncover that hidden gem as you wander in the shadow of the castle.

# Nightclubs

## THE GAY SCENE

Edinburgh has a vibrant gay scene that centres around Broughton Street, an area known as the Pink Triangle. Hotels, clubs, cafés and pubs cater for the gay community. For pre-club drinks try the popular Blue Moon Café (✉ 36 Broughton Street EH1 3SB ☎ 0131 557 0911), the longest-running gay gathering place, or the Planet Out (✉ 6 Baxter's Place EH1 3AF ☎ 0131 556 5551) is a lively bar with a great atmosphere. Serious clubbers head to The Venue (▶ 84) for 'Joy', the best gay night in Edinburgh. Also popular is CC Blooms (✉ 23 Greenside Place EH1 3AA ☎ 0131 556 9331), a big brash place but lots of fun.

## BELUGA

Opulent and stylish restaurant by day where the basement bar evolves into a heaving dance floor by night. Leather seats and metal fittings, dominated by a huge waterfall.

➕ F9 ✉ 30a Chambers Street EH1 1HU ☎ 0131 624 4545 🕐 Daily 10am–1am 🚌 23, 27, 35

## BONGO CLUB

Popular and chilled hot spot that boasts interesting club nights, covering different genres of music, from funk and house to jazz and rare grooves.

➕ G9 ✉ Moray House, 37 Holyrood Road EH8 8AQ ☎ 0131 556 5204 🕐 Mon–Sun 10pm–3am 🚌 35

## CITY NIGHTCLUB

Amazing sports bar and nightclub in the basement of the Scotsman Hotel, which has become Edinburgh's most talked about late-night venue. A mix of music styles to suit all dancing fanatics.

➕ F8 ✉ 1a Market Street EH1 1DE ☎ 0131 224 9560 🕐 Bar: Mon–Sat 11am–3am, Sun 12.30pm–3am. Club: Fri, Sat 11pm–3am, Wed 10.30pm–3am, Thu 11pm–3am 🚌 3, 5, 7, 30, 31, 33, 37

## ESPIONAGE

Dance the night away at this popular complex, with its four spy-themed bars and two dance floors.

➕ F9 ✉ 9 Victoria Street EH1 1EX ☎ 0131 477 7007 🕐 Nightly 7pm–3am (to 5am during Festival) 🚌 2, 23, 27, 35, 41, 42

## HONEYCOMBE

A seriously cool clientele flocks to this classy haunt for great house nights. Padded walls, a chic steel bar and intimate dance floor set the scene.

➕ F9 ✉ 15–17 Niddry Street EH1 1LG ☎ 0131 556 2442 🕐 Nightly 10.30pm–3am 🚌 3, 5, 7, 14, 29, 30, 31, 33, 37, 49

## LIQUID ROOM

Subterranean basement club that pulls in the punters to its renowned resident club night, which features big names like Roger Sanchez and Sasha.

➕ F9 ✉ 9c Victoria Street EH1 2HE ☎ 0131 225 2564 🕐 Nightly 10.30pm–3am 🚌 2, 23, 27, 35, 41

## OPAL LOUNGE

The multi-purpose basement space is stylish but casual, and subtly evolves through the day from food to drinking to dancing to funky, soul infused tunes.

➕ E8 ✉ 51 George Street EH2 2HT ☎ 0131 226 2275 🕐 Daily noon–3am 🚌 13, 19, 37, 41

## SUBWAY

One of Edinburgh's top clubs and most certainly the busiest, playing all the best from 1960s to '90s music; also live emerging bands.

➕ F9 ✉ 69 The Cowgate EH1 1JW ☎ 0131 225 6766 🕐 Mon–Sun 5pm–5am 🚌 2, 23, 27, 41, 42, 45

# Pubs & Bars

### BAILLIE BAR
Sample real ales at this New Town basement pub with an interesting triangular-shaped bar, low ceilings and lavish dark-red walls.

✚ D7 ✉ 2 St. Stephen Street EH3 5AL ☎ 0131 225 4673 🚌 13, 19, 24, 29, 42

### BOW BAR
If it's a wee dram you're after, this traditional pub is *the* place for whisky, with over 140 malts. Wood panelling, old brewery mirrors and a warm greeting creates an authentic atmosphere.

✚ F9 ✉ 80 West Bow EH1 2HH ☎ 0131 226 7667 🚌 23, 27, 35, 41

### CAFÉ ROYAL CIRCLE
Stop by for a drink and admire the ornate ceiling, tiled portraits, stained glass and mahogany carvings, but its huge circular bar takes centre stage.

✚ F8 ✉ 19 West Register Street EH2 2AA ☎ 0131 556 1884 🚌 3, 10, 17, 23, 24, 27, 44 and others

### CASK AND BARREL
Staff who know their stuff serve the real ales at this conventional pub. If you're not into football don't come on the day of a big match; it's standing room only as locals flock to watch the game.

✚ F7 ✉ 115 Broughton Street EH1 3RZ ☎ 0131 556 3132 🚌 8, 17

### FISH TANK
Discrete hideaway on the corner of Hanover and Queen streets, and one of the coolest pre-club hang outs. The relaxed and intimate bar hosts DJ slots and has a mini dance floor.

✚ E8 ✉ 16a Queen Street EH2 1JE ☎ 0131 226 5959 🚌 12, 13, 15, 23, 27, 29, 42

### GRAPE
Chic wine bar with a big selection of wines. The comfy sofas provide an equally good coffee break during the day.

✚ F8 ✉ The Capital Building, 13 St. Andrew Square EH2 2BH ☎ 0131 557 4522 🚌 8, 10, 11, 12, 16

### GREYFRIARS BOBBY
In front of Greyfriars Kirk and named after the famous loyal dog, this wooden-fronted building houses a traditional friendly pub, popular with students and visitors alike.

✚ F9 ✉ 34 Candlemaker Row EH1 2QE ☎ 0131 225 8328 🚌 27, 35, 41, 42

### JOLLY JUDGE
Delightful little pub with 17th-century character, including a low-beamed ceiling and a wide choice of malt whiskies. Difficult to find but worth the search.

✚ F9 ✉ 7 James Court, off Lawnmarket EH1 2PB ☎ 0131 225 2669 🚌 23, 27, 35, 41, 42

### RICK'S
Rick's is a cocktail bar, restaurant and rooms all in one. The sophisticated basement bar rocks from 10pm until 1am.

✚ E8 ✉ 55a Frederick Street EH2 1LH ☎ 0131 622 7800 🚌 13, 19, 24, 29, 37, 42

### LICENSING LAWS
In the 1980s, Edinburgh was one of the first cities in Britain to pioneer pubs staying open all day. These new licensing laws proved to be a great success, bringing about an immediate drop in alcohol-related street disturbance in the area. Pubs can serve alcohol 11am–11pm from Monday to Saturday and 12.30–2.30 and 6.30–11 on Sundays, although a regular extension may allow premises to stay open longer. Not many Edinburgh pubs cater specifically for acccompanied children, though outside the city they will be welcome if you are having a pub meal– children age 16–18 can drink alcohol if they have ordered a meal.

# Cinemas

## EDINBURGH INTERNATIONAL FILM FESTIVAL

This is the world's longest-running film festival, having produced innovative and exciting cinema since 1947. Its beginnings lie in documentary film, evolving into a pioneering force for the world of cinema. Held every year in August and running consecutively with the Fringe, it is a celebration of cinema and a showcase for new films from all over the world, as well as presenting UK and world premieres, video shorts and animation. The festival takes place across Edinburgh's cinemas and runs for two weeks. For information contact the Edinburgh International Film Festival (✉ 88 Lothian Road EH3 9BZ ☎ 0131 228 4051; 0131 229 2550 (information line); 0131 623 8030 (tickets); www.edfilmfest.org).

## CAMEO

Small, comfortable cinema showing low-key Hollywood, international and independent films.
➕ D10 ✉ 38 Home Street EH3 9LZ ☎ 0131 228 4141 (box office); 0131 228 2800 (24-hour recorded information); www.picturehouse.co.uk
🚌 10, 11, 15, 16, 17, 23, 37

## DOMINION

This old-fashioned, family-run cinema is the ideal antidote to the multiplex cinemas that are engulfing the city. View latest releases in leather Pullman seats, or indulge in the Gold Class service, which offers leather sofas with complimentary wine or beer and snacks.
➕ C13 ✉ 18 Newbattle Terrace, Morningside EH10 4RT ☎ 0131 447 4771 (box office); 0131 447 2660 (recorded information); www.dominioncinema.com
🚌 11, 15, 16, 23

## FILMHOUSE

Opposite the Usher Hall, this art-house cinema has three screens that feature the best in art-house and foreign language cinema from around the globe.
➕ C9 ✉ 88 Lothian Road EH3 9BZ ☎ 0131 228 2688 (enquiries); 0131 228 2689 (recorded information); www.filmhousecinema.com
🚌 10, 11, 15, 17, 17, 34, 35

## ODEON

Centrally located five-screen cinema with the latest sound sytems, showing all the big mainstream movies.
➕ D10 ✉ 118 Lothian Road EH3 8BG ☎ 0871 224 4007; www.odeon.co.uk 🚌 10, 11, 15, 16, 17

## STER CENTURY

All the latest releases are screened at this state-of-the-art 12-screen multiplex, with the latest in digital surround sound and comfortable seats that give extra leg room. Free parking.
➕ H2 ✉ Ocean Terminal, Ocean Drive, Leith EH6 7DZ ☎ 0131 553 0700; www.stercentury.co.uk
🚌 1, 11, 22, 34, 35

## UCI

A modern complex in a retail park on the outskirts of Edinburgh, with 12 screens showing a large range of mainstream movies.
➕ Off map ✉ 7 Kinnaird Park, Newcraighall Road EH15 3RD M10 ☎ 0131 669 0777 (enquiries); 08700 102 030 (recorded information); www.uci.co.uk 🚌 30; First Bus 141, 142

## VUE

A huge glass-fronted multiplex cinema with 12 screens and the latest technology, which ensures a wide selection of current releases are showing at one time. A Gold Class ticket gives you extra luxuries such as leather seats and waiter bar service.
➕ G7 ✉ Omni Leisure Building, Greenside Place, Leith Street EH1 3EN ☎ 08712 240 240 (enquiries); 08702 406020 (24-hour recorded information and card bookings); www.myvue.com 🚌 1, 5, 7, 14, 19, 22

# Theatres

### CHURCH HILL THEATRE

Mainly amateur productions but professionals perform during the Festival.
➕ C13 ✉ 33 Morningside Road EH10 4RR ☎ 0131 447 7597 🚌 5, 11, 15, 16, 17, 23

### EDINBURGH FESTIVAL THEATRE

The distinctive glass façade conceals one of the largest stages in Europe. Full programme of international dance, theatre, variety and comedy, from contemporary ballet to performances from the Scottish Opera.
➕ F9 ✉ 13–29 Nicolson Street EH8 9FT ☎ 0131 529 6000; www.eft.co.uk 🚌 2, 3, 5, 7, 8, 14, 29, 30, 31, 33, 37, 49

### EDINBURGH PLAYHOUSE

A multi-purpose auditorium that presents big-budget musicals and dance, and concerts featuring leading rock groups. Close to the east end of Princes Street.
➕ G7 ✉ 18–22 Greenside Place EH1 3AA ☎ 0131 524 3333; ticketmaster 0870 606 3424 (24 hours); www.getlive.co.uk 🚌 7, 10, 11, 12, 14, 22, 25, 26, 49

### KING'S THEATRE

One of Edinburgh's oldest theatres, housed in a handsome Edwardian building. Diverse programme of shows and musicals, pantomime, comedy, plays—including Shakespeare—and international opera during the festival.

➕ D10 ✉ 2 Leven Street EH3 9LQ ☎ 0131 529 6000; www.eft.co.uk 🚌 11, 15, 16, 17, 23

### SCOTTISH STORY-TELLING CENTRE

Refurbished to provide more capacity for its Scottish and children's theatre, and story and poetry readings.
➕ G9 ✉ 43–45 High Street EH1 1SR ☎ 0131 556 9579; www.scottishstorytellingcentre.co.uk 🚌 35 and all North Bridge buses

### ROSS OPEN AIR THEATRE

Impressive spot for a summer programme of major outdoor concerts and live events, beneath Edinburgh Castle.
➕ E9 ✉ Princes Street Gardens ☎ 0131 228 1155 🚌 3, 10, 17, 23, 24, 27, 44 & others

### ROYAL LYCEUM THEATRE

A magnificent Victorian theatre that creates all its own shows. Contemporary and classic productions feature, as well as new works.
➕ D9 ✉ Grindlay Street EH3 9AX ☎ 0131 248 4848; www.lyceum.org.uk 🚌 1, 10, 11, 15, 16, 17, 22, 34

### TRAVERSE THEATRE

State-of-the-art venue next to the Usher Hall, respected for its experimental theatre and dance productions; you can see hot new work by Scottish playwrights.
➕ D9 ✉ 10 Cambridge Street EH1 2ED ☎ 0131 228 1404; www.traverse.co.uk 🚌 10, 11, 22

### JUST FOR LAUGHS

It's easy to forget that not so long ago, once the glut of the Edinburgh Fringe had come and gone, the Scottish comedy scene was a patchy affair. But thanks primarily to the efforts of the Stand Comedy Club (✉ 5 York Place EH1 3EB ☎ 0131 558 7272; www.thestand.co.uk 🚌 10, 11, 12, 15, 16, 17, 26, 44), a genuine circuit has re-emerged, helping talented comics to flourish. At this dark intimate basement bar you can enjoy well-known Scottish comedians and promising new talent, seven nights a week.

# Live Music

## CELTIC MUSIC

Edinburgh pubs and dinner shows (► this page) are the best places to track down a genuine Celtic music session. Celtic music originates from the seven Celtic countries—Scotland, Ireland, Wales, Isle of Man, Cornwall, Brittany and Galicia. The following city pubs have fine singers and musicians performing on a regular basis: Sandy Bells Bar (✉ Forrest Road EH1 2QH ☎ 0131 225 2751); The Tass (✉ corner of High Street and St. Mary's Street EH1 1SR ☎ 0131 556 6338); The Royal Oak (✉ Infirmary Street EH1 1LT ☎ 0131 557 2976). Dates and times can be erratic, so check first before you venture forth.

## ASSEMBLY ROOMS

Elegant Georgian building showcasing mainstream Festival Fringe productions, with an impressive ballroom and music hall.
➕ E8 ✉ 50 George Street EH2 2LE ☎ 0131 624 2442; www.assemblyrooms.com
🚌 19, 37, 41

## EDINBURGH CORN EXCHANGE

Pop and rock venue where acts have included well-known bands such as Blur, Travis and Coldplay.
➕ Off map at A14 ✉ 11 New Market Road EH14 1RJ ☎ 0131 447 3500; www.ece.uk.com
🚌 35 🚆 Slateford from Waverley

## GEORGE SCOTTISH EVENING

Relax over a fine five-course meal in opulent surroundings while enjoying traditional Scottish entertainment. Reserve ahead.
➕ E8 ✉ Adam Room, George InterContinental Hotel, 19–21 George Street EH2 2PB ☎ 0131 225 1251 🕐 Jun–end Sep Sun, Wed, Fri 🚌 13, 19, 37, 41, 42

## HENRY'S JAZZ BAR

Pioneering jazz venue draws quality acts from around the world. Dimmed lights, red walls and candles set the tone for contemporary jazz performers.
➕ D10 ✉ 8 Morrison Street EH3 8BJ ☎ 0131 467 5200; www.jazzmusic.co.uk 🚌 2

## JAMIE'S SCOTTISH EVENING

This delightful dinner show, hosted by the Thistle Hotel, has entertained audiences with Scottish dancing, singing and bagpipes for over 25 years.
➕ F8 ✉ Thistle Hotel, 107 Leith Street EH1 3SW ☎ 0131 556 0111 🕐 Apr–Nov nightly from 7pm 🚌 1, 5, 7, 14, 19, 22, 25, 34

## QUEEN'S HALL

In a converted church, this intimate venue is the spot for a range of events from jazz and blues to rock and classical music, and comedy from top class performers. Home to the Scottish Chamber Orchestra.
➕ G11 ✉ 89 Clerk Street EH8 9JG ☎ 0131 668 2019; www.queenshalledinburgh.co.uk
🚌 3, 5, 7, 8, 29, 31, 37

## USHER HALL

The copper dome of this distinctive circular concert hall is a familiar sight from many parts of the city. A prestigious venue, which attracts the very best performers like José Carreras, the English Chamber Orchestra and the Moscow Philharmonic.
➕ D9 ✉ Lothian Road EH1 2EA ☎ 0131 228 1155; www.usherhall.co.uk 🚌 1, 10, 11, 15, 16, 17, 22, 24, 34

## THE VENUE

Intimate club/gig venue where up-and-coming rock, funk, pop and indie bands strut their stuff on the large stage. Near Waverley station.
➕ F8 ✉ 15–21 Calton Road EH8 8DL ☎ 0131 557 3073 🚌 All buses to Waverley station, then few minutes walk

# Sport & Activities

## SPECTATOR SPORTS

### FOOTBALL

Edinburgh's two main professional teams are Heart of Midlothian (Hearts) and Hibernian (Hibs), who play in the Scottish Premier League. You will find them at home on alternate Saturday afternoons Aug–May (reserve in advance).

**Hearts FC** ✚ Off map at A12 ✉ Tynecastle Stadium, Gorgie Road EH11 2NL ☎ 0131 200 7201; www.heartsfc.co.uk 🚌 3, 3a, 25, 33

**Hibs FC** ✚ J6 ✉ Easter Road Stadium, 12 Albion Place EH7 5QG ☎ 0131 661 1875; www.hibs.co.uk 🚌 1

### HORSE RACING

Musselburgh Racecourse, one of the best small racecourses in Britain, hosts 20 flat and jump meetings a year.

✚ Off map at M9 ✉ Linkfield Road, Musselburgh, East Lothian ☎ 0131 665 2859; www.musselburgh-racecourse.co.uk 🚌 15, 15A

### RUGBY

Rugby is one of Edinburgh's favourite sports. Murrayfield Stadium, 1.5km (1 mile) west of the heart of the city, is home to the Scottish national team and international games are well supported; it is essential to reserve ahead. Stadium tours available.

✚ Off map at A10 ✉ Murrayfield Stadium, Corstorphine Road EH12 5PJ ☎ 0131 3465000; www.sru.org.uk 🚌 12, 26, 31

## PARTICIPANT SPORTS

### BICYCLING

Rent a bicycle and explore the city on two wheels. Bike Trax have a vast selection of mountain and touring bicycles available for rental.

**Bike Trax** ✚ D10 ✉ 7–11 Lochrin Place, Tollcross EH3 9QX ☎ 0131 228 6633; www.biketrax.co.uk 🚌 1, 10, 11, 15, 16, 17, 34, 35

### GOLF

Golf is the national game and with more than 500 courses throughout the country, it's no wonder fanatics flock to the area in pursuit of their first love. Visit www.scottishgolf.com for a list of courses and a reservation service. Here are a few close at hand.

**Braid Hills** ✚ Off map at C15 ✉ 22 Braid Hills Approach EH10 6JY ☎ 0131 452 9408 🚌 11, 15, 15A

**Craigmillar Park** ✚ G14 ✉ 1 Observatory Road EH9 3HG ☎ 0131 667 0047 🚌 38

**Silverknowes** ✚ Off map at A4 ✉ Silverknowes Parkway EH4 5ET ☎ 0131 336 5359 🚌 16, 27, 42

### SWIMMING

Edinburgh is proud of its Olympic-size indoor swimming pool, complete with a diving pool and waterslides. For further fun swimming try Leith Waterworld (► 59)

**Royal Commonwealth Pool** ✚ H11 ✉ 21 Dalkeith Road EH16 5BB ☎ 0131 667 7211; www.edinburgh.gov.uk 🚌 2, 14, 30, 33

### OTHER ACTIVITIES

Edinburgh offers some of the country's best facilities for a diverse range of sports and activities. If ice-skating is your passion visit the Murrayfield Ice Rink (✉ Riversdale Crescent EH12 5XN ☎ 0131 337 6933), home to the Capitals, Edinburgh's ice-hockey team. Skiing enthusiasts will enjoy the Midlothian Ski Centre (✉ Hillend EH10 7DU ☎ 0131 445 4433), which has the longest artificial slope in Europe. Port Edgar Sailing School (✉ Shore Road, South Queensferry EH30 9SQ ☎ 0131 331 3330) is the largest watersport centre in Scotland. If you want a game of tennis try the Craiglockhart Sports Centre (✉ 177 Colinton Road EH14 1BZ ☎ 0131 443 0101), which offers indoor and outdoor courts, as well as other racket sports.

# Luxury Hotels

## PRICES

Expect to pay the following prices for a double room per night:

Luxury over £140
Mid-range £75–£140
Budget under £75

## PEACE AND QUIET

After spending a few days exploring Edinburgh's environs, you may be tempted to take to the countryside for some peace and quiet. Dalhousie Castle and Spa (✉ Bonnyrigg EH19 3JB ☎ 01875 820153; fax 0131 01875 821936; www.dalhousiecastle.co.uk) can provide just that, plus luxurious pampering. This magnificent 13th-century castle amid manicured lawns and parkland, is about 11km (7 miles) outside Edinburgh. The 36 themed rooms are named after historical figures and are opulently decorated. Facilities include two restaurants, and a sauna and spa.

### BALMORAL

An impressive landmark in the heart of the city. After a major facelift, the 188 bedrooms now have a contemporary feel with neutral tones, while retaining the Balmoral's grandeur.
✚ F8 ✉ 1 Princes Street EH2 2EQ ☎ 0131 556 2414; fax 0131 557 3747; www.roccofortehotels.com ▣ 3, 10, 17, 23, 24, 27, 44 and others

### THE BONHAM

A West End hotel that offers bright modern-day rooms with mood lighting and striking art, and 48 bedrooms combining high standards of style with 21st-century technology.
✚ C8 ✉ 35 Drumsheugh Gardens EH3 7RN ☎ 0131 623 9301; fax 0131 332 9631; www.thebonham.com ▣ 13

### BRUNTSFIELD HOTEL

Overlooking Bruntsfield Links, this chic hotel has stylish lounge areas and 73 bedrooms varying in size. Meals are served in a conservatory-style restaurant.
✚ D11 ✉ 69–74 Bruntsfield Place EH10 4HH ☎ 0131 229 1393; fax 0131 229 5634; www.thebruntsfield.co.uk ▣ 16, 17, 23

### GLASSHOUSE

Modern glass architecture embraces a striking church façade as you enter this chic boutique hotel. The 65 rooms have floor-to-ceiling windows that ensure spectacular views over Calton Hill, and ooze luxury with a contemporary edge. Rooftop bar and garden.
✚ G7 ✉ 2 Greenside Place EH1 3AA ☎ 0131 525 8200; fax 0131 525 8205; www.theetoncollection.com ▣ 4, 7, 10, 11, 12, 16, 22, 34

### THE HOWARD

Three Georgian houses make up this sophisticated hotel, a short walk from Princes Street. The 18 good-sized rooms have bathrooms with claw-foot baths, and the elegant day rooms are decked out with chandeliers, lavish drapes and painted murals.
✚ E7 ✉ 34 Great King Street EH3 6QH ☎ 0131 623 9303; fax 0131 623 9306; www.thehoward.com ▣ 13

### MALMAISON

Stylish hotel with 100 bedrooms; some in bold stripes, others in subtle tones; some have views of the harbour at Leith.
✚ J3 ✉ 1 Tower Place, Leith EH6 7DB ☎ 0131 468 5000; fax 0131 468 5002; www.malmaison.com ▣ 16, 22, 35, 36

### THE SCOTSMAN

Once head office to *The Scotsman* newspaper in the Old Town, but now transformed into a state-of-the-art hotel, where classic elegance blends with high-tech design. The 68 rooms are in various sizes and styles. Unusual stainless steel swimming pool.
✚ F8 ✉ 20 North Bridge EH1 1YT ☎ 0131 556 5565; fax 0131 652 3652; www.thescotsmanhotel.co.uk ▣ 3, 5, 7, 30, 31, 33, 37

# Mid-Range Hotels

### CHANNINGS

Friendly town house with traditional elegance, which offers country-style tranquillity in a West End setting. The 46 rooms vary in size but all are decorated with style.

➕ B7 ✉ South Learmonth Gardens EH4 1EZ ☎ 0131 623 9302; fax 0131 322 9631; www.channings.co.uk 🚌 19, 37

### DALMAHOY HOTEL MARRIOTT & COUNTRY CLUB

An imposing Georgian mansion in beautiful parkland, 11km (7 miles) southwest of the city. Most of the 215 spacious bedrooms have great views of the Pentland Hills. Guests have the use of two golf courses and a health and beauty club.

➕ Off map at A11 ✉ Kirknewton EH27 8EB ☎ 0131 333 1845; fax 0131 333 1433; www.marriott.com

### DUNSTANE HOUSE

In the city's West End close to Haymarket station, this splendid 1850's Victorian mansion house has retained much of its architectural grandeur, lending an intimate country house atmosphere. Some of the 60 bedrooms have four-poster beds.

➕ B10 ✉ 4 West Coates, Haymarket EH12 5JQ ☎ 0131 337 6169; fax 0131 337 6060; www.dunstane-hotel-edinburgh.co.uk 🚌 12, 26, 31

### HOLYROOD HOTEL

This impressive business hotel, next to the new Scottish Parliament Building, offers extensive facilities including conference suites and a spa. There are 156 rooms.

➕ H8 ✉ Holyrood Road EH8 6AE ☎ 0131 550 4500; fax 0131 550 4545; www.macdonaldhotels.co.uk 🚌 35

### KILDONAN LODGE

Small hotel with 12 beautifully restored bedrooms—some with four-posters and spas—in an elegant Victorian house, where nothing is too much trouble. Pre-dinner drinks can be taken in the lounge in front of an open fire.

➕ J14 ✉ 27 Craigmillar Park EH16 5PE ☎ 0131 667 2793; fax 0131 667 9777; www.kildonanlodgehotel.co.uk 🚌 3, 7, 8, 29, 37, 37a, 49

### NEWINGTON COTTAGE

Deceptively spacious bed-and-breakfast close to Holyrood Park. Pretty public areas are adorned with flowers. The three bedrooms include extras such as a fridge, CD player, fresh fruit and a decanter of sherry. No children under 13.

➕ H12 ✉ 15 Blacket Place EH9 1RJ ☎ 0131 668 1935; fax 0131 667 4644; www.newcot.demon.co.uk 🚌 3, 7, 8, 29, 37, 37a, 49

### POINT HOTEL

A distinctive structure shadowed by the castle, this 140-room hotel blends elegance with minimalist design.

➕ D10 ✉ 34 Bread Street EH3 9AF ☎ 0131 221 5555; fax 0131 221 9929; www.point-hotel.co.uk 🚌 2

### STAR GRADING

You may notice that displayed outside all Scottish accommodation is a blue plaque with a thistle symbol. This indicates the star rating issued by VisitScotland (Scottish Tourist Board). Every type of accommodation is assessed annually and awarded anything from one to five stars to distinguish between the quality of accommodation, cleanlinesss, ambience, hospitality, service and food, and facilities offered.

# Budget Hotels

## TYPES OF ACCOMMODATION

Apart from the larger more obvious hotels, Edinburgh has numerous guest houses and small family-run hotels. The latter will have more rooms, normally all with en suite facilities; they will probably be licensed to serve alcohol and they will provide breakfast, dinner and sometimes lunch. For something more home-like, bed-and-breakfasts are usually very comfortable, and give you the opportunity to sample a real Scottish breakfast. If you intend to stay outside the city, it's worth considering self-catering accommodation. The options vary from a pretty cottage or a grand castle to an apartment or chalet. There are several holiday parks nearby that offer holiday homes and touring caravan and camping pitches to suit the lower budget.

### ABBOTSFORD GUEST HOUSE

Just north of New Town, this family-run guest house has eight individual and well-equipped bedrooms. Elegant dining room.
✚ G5 ✉ 36 Pilrig Street EH6 5AL ☎ 0131 554 2706; www.abbotsfordguesthouse.co.uk ▣ 11

### BONNINGTON GUEST HOUSE

The owners extend a warm welcome at this delightful Georgian house not far from Leith, with six bedrooms finished to a high standard and retaining original features.
✚ F4 ✉ 202 Ferry Road EH6 4NW ☎ 0131 554 7610; www.bonnington-guest-house-edinburgh.co.uk ▣ 7, 14

### DENE GUESTHOUSE

Hospitable owners offer a comfortable stay and a good breakfast at this clean and tidy Georgian town house. Well-sited in New Town, making it ideal for visiting the city's main sites.
✚ E6 ✉ 7 Eyre Place EH3 5ES ☎ 0131 556 2700; fax 0131 557 9876; www.deneguesthouse.com ▣ 23, 27, 36

### THE EGLINTON

Smart accommodation in a fine Georgian West End property. The 12 comfortable bedrooms vary in size; the larger ones are extremely elegant. Small bar.
✚ B9 ✉ 29 Eglinton Crescent EH12 5BY ☎ 0131 337 2641; fax 0131 337 4495; www.eglinton-hotel.co.uk ▣ 26, 31

### ELMVIEW

Part of a stylish Victorian terrace on the edge of Old Town, the three bedrooms have fridges containing fresh milk and water, and smart bathrooms. Breakfast is served at one large communal table. No smoking and no children under 15.
✚ E11 ✉ 15 Glengyle Terrace EH3 9LN ☎ 0131 228 1973; www.elmview.co.uk ▣ 24, 41

### IVY HOUSE

Pretty guest house south of the city. The eight bedrooms come in various sizes. Good substantial breakfasts.
✚ H13 ✉ 7 Mayfield Gardens EH9 2AX ☎ 0131 667 3411; fax 0131 620 1422; www.ivyguesthouse.com ▣ 3, 7, 8, 29, 31, 37, 49, 37a

### KEW HOUSE

Spotless throughout, Kew House has six bright bedrooms and a comfortable lounge offering supper and snack options. Near Murrayfield Stadium. No smoking.
✚ Off map at A10 ✉ 1 Kew Terrace, Murrayfield EH12 5JE ☎ 0131 313 0700; fax 0131 313 0747; www.kewhouse.com ▣ 12, 26, 31

### THE STUARTS

Overlooking a tree-filled park south of Old Town, this immaculate guest house offers three spacious bedrooms with luxury bathrooms—all with hi-fi, video and a fridge. No smoking.
✚ E11 ✉ 17 Glengyle Terrace EH3 9LN ☎ 0131 229 9559; www.the-stuarts.com ▣ 24, 41

# EDINBURGH
## travel facts

## ESSENTIAL FACTS

### Customs regulations

- EU nationals do not have to declare goods imported for their own use, although you may be questioned by customs officials if you have large amounts of certain items.
- The limits for non-EU visitors are 200 cigarettes or 50 cigars or 250g of tobacco; 1 litre of alcohol (over 22 per cent alcohol) or 2 litres of wine; 50g of perfume.

### Electricity

- Britain is on 240 volts AC, and plugs have three square pins. If you are bringing an electrical appliance from another country where the voltage is the same, a plug adaptor will suffice. If the voltage is different, as in the US—110 volts—you need a converter.
- Small appliances such as razors can run on a 50-watt converter, while heating appliances, irons and hair-dryers require a 1,600-watt converter.

### Etiquette

It is customary to tip the following:
- Restaurants (where service is not included) 10–15 per cent
- Tour guides £1–£2
- Taxis 10 per cent
- Hairdressers 10 per cent
- Chambermaids 50p–£1 per day
- Porters 50p–£1 per bag

### Money and credit cards

- Credit cards are widely accepted.
- ATMs are widely available.

### National holidays

- New Year's Day (1 January)
- New Year's Holiday (2 January)
- Good Friday
- Easter Monday
- First Monday in May
- Last Monday in May
- First Monday in August
- Last Monday in August
- Christmas Day (25 December)
- Boxing Day (26 December)
- Most places of interest close on New Year's Day, 1 May and Christmas, while others close on all public holidays.

### Opening times

- Banks: Mon–Fri 9.30–4.30; larger branches may open Sat am.
- Post offices: Mon–Fri 9–5.30, Sat 9–noon.
- Shops: Mon–Sat 9–5 or 5.30. Newsagents and some shops may open on Sun.
- Museums: opening times vary widely, see individual entries.

### Student travellers

- Students can get reduced-cost entry to some museums and attractions by showing a valid student card. There are some good budget accommodation and hostels available.
- There are reduced fares on buses and trains for under 16s.

### Toilets

- Generally these are well-located, plentiful and free in built-up areas. There may be a small charge to use toilets at some rail stations.
- It is not acceptable for those who are not customers to use the toilets in pubs, cafés and restaurants. Buy a drink first.

### Tourist information office

- The official source of information for tourists is VisitScotland, which has a very useful website www.visitscotland.com and National Booking and Information

service ☎ 0845 22 55 121.
- Edinburgh and Scotland Information Centre, Princes Mall, 3 Princes Street, EH2 2QP ☎ 0131 473 3800 ⦿ May, Jun, Sep Mon–Sat 9–7, Sun 10–7; Jul, Aug Mon–Sat 9–8, Sun 10–8; Oct–end April Mon–Sat 9–6, Sun 10–6
- Edinburgh Airport Tourist Information Desk, Ingliston EH12 9DN ⦿ Apr–end Oct Mon–Sat 6.30am–10.30pm; Nov–end Mar daily 7.30am–9.30pm.

## GETTING AROUND

For public transport ➤ 6–7

### Car rental

- Major rental firms such as Avis, Hertz and Budget have offices at Edinburgh Airport ☎ 0131 333 1000. There are also local firms including Arnold Clark ☎ 0845 60 745 00 and Edinburgh Self Drive ☎ 0131 229 6333.

### Edinburgh Pass

- Launched in spring 2005, this card gives free access to more than 25 attractions in Edinburgh and the Lothians. It also includes free bus travel, including airport bus transfer, and offers from some shops, restaurants and Festival events. A free guidebook explains what's on offer. Cost: 1-day pass £26, 2-day £34 and 3-day £40. You can buy online at www.edinburgh pass.org or purchase from the Tourist Information Centres at the airport or in the city.

## MEDIA & COMMUNICATIONS

### Newspapers and Magazines

- *The Scotsman* is at the quality end of the market.
- Scotland's popular tabloid daily newspaper is the *Daily Record*.

- The *Sunday Post* is a top-selling institution.
- *Scotland on Sunday* is a heavyweight that vies with the *Sunday Herald* for the more serious readership.
- *The List* is a lively fortnightly listings magazine, giving excellent coverage for Edinburgh
- Newspapers from around the world, including foreign-language papers, can be purchased at airports, larger train stations and some newspaper shops.

### Post offices

- Main post office ✉ St. James Centre, St. Andrew Square ☎ 0131 556 0478 ⦿ Mon–Fri 9–5.30, Sat 8.30–6. Most other post offices open 9–12.30 on Sat.
- Many newspaper shops and supermarkets sell stamps.
- Postboxes are painted red; collection times are shown on each box.

### Radio and Television

- Scotland is served by the UK's national radio stations (BBC), and has some of its own for more Scottish coverage.
- BBC Radio Scotland has a loyal following; it broadcasts a broad mix of news, discussion, travel, magazine format and music shows, and is useful for weather forecasts.
- There are also several local radio stations for news bulletins, and commerical stations including Radio Forth (serving Edinburgh).
- There are five main national terrestrial TV channels in Britain. Scotland's mainstream television choice is essentially what is broadcast from south of the border, with local interest, home-based material slotted in.

- Satellite television, dominated by Sky TV, is widely available, sometimes bringing TV to regions that had trouble with terrestrial reception in the past.

## Telephones

- The code for Edinburgh is 0131. There is a full list of area codes and country codes in all phone books. Omit the area code when making a local call.
- Phone cards for payphones can be used in units of £2, £5 and £10. Coins of 10p, 20p, 50p and £1 are also accepted. Credit and debit cards can be used to make calls from many BT (British Telecom) payphones (50p minimum charge; 20p per minute for all inland calls). Pay-phones in hotels and pubs can be very expensive as the venues set their own profit margin.
- Directory enquiries have companies competing for services. The BT numbers are:
- Directory Enquiries ☎ 118 500
- International directory enquiries ☎ 118 505
- Other services:
- International operator ☎ 155
- Operator ☎ 100
- Cheap rate is after 6pm weekdays and all day Saturday and Sunday.
- To call the US from Scotland dial 00 1, followed by the number.
- To call Scotland from the US, dial 011 44, then omit the 0 from the area code.

## EMERGENCIES

### Consulates

- All embassies are located in London but the following consulates are based in Edinburgh:
- French Consulate ✉ 11 Randolph Crescent EH3 7TT ☎ 0131 225 7954

- German Consulate ✉ 16 Eglinton Crescent EH12 5DG ☎ 0131 337 2323
- Netherlands Consulate ✉ Thistle Court, 1–2 Thistle Street EH2 1DD ☎ 0131 220 3226
- Spanish Consulate ✉ 63 North Castle Street EH2 3LJ ☎ 0131 220 1843
- US Consulate ✉ 3 Regent Terrace EH7 5BW ☎ 0131 556 8315

### Emergency telephone numbers

- Police, Ambulance, Fire ☎ 999 or 112.
- For non-emergency police enquiries contact the nearest police station (see directory enquiries ► this page).
- If you break down driving your own car you can call the Automobile Association and join on the spot if you are not already a member (☎ 0800 887766). Check if your home country membership entitles you to reciprocal assistance. If you are driving a rental car, call the emergency number given in your documentation.

### Lost property

- Property found and handed to the police is sent to Police Head-quarters ✉ Fettes Avenue ☎ 0131 311 3131 🕐 Mon–Fri 9–5.
- There are lost property departments at Edinburgh Airport ☎ 0131 344 3486; Waverley train station ☎ 0131 550 2333; and Lothian buses ✉ Annandale Street, off Leith Walk ☎ 0131 558 8858 🕐 Mon–Fri 10–1.30
- Report losses of passports to the police.

## Medicines and medical treatment

- Citizens from the EU are entitled to free or reduced-cost NHS (National Health Service) treatment—bring the E111 form (or EHIC from 2006) from your home country. Full health and travel insurance is still advised. Those travelling from outside the EU should have full travel and health insurance.
- For medical emergencies ☎ 999 or 112 or go to the nearest hospital casualty department (emergency room). The 24-hour casualty department is at the Royal Infirmary of Edinburgh ✉ 1 Lauriston Place ☎ 0131 536 1000. For minor injuries the Western General Hospital ✉ Crewe Road ☎ 0131 537 1330 has a walk-in service ◐ Daily 9–9
- To find the nearest doctor, dentist or pharmacy ask at your hotel or look up the website www.nhs.uk/local services.
- Dental: an emergency service for the relief of pain only is available at the Casualty Department of the Edinburgh Dental Institute ✉ Lauriston Place ☎ 0131 536 4958 ◐ Mon–Fri 9–3, 7–7, weekends 10–12. There is a walk-in centre and emergency clinic at the Western General Hospital ✉ Crewe Road ☎ 0131 536 4958 ◐ Mon–Fri 9–3.30 (also emergencies daily 7pm–9pm, also Sat, Sun 10am–noon). Make sure you have a means of payment with you. Standard NHS charges will be made.
- Pharmacies and large super-markets have a range of medicines available over the counter but items such as antibiotics require a doctor's prescription.
- There are no 24-hour pharmacies in Edinburgh. Boots the Chemist ✉ 48 Shandwick Place ☎ 0131 225 6757 has the longest opening hours ◐ Mon–Fri 8am–9pm, Sat 8am–7pm, Sun 10am–5pm.

## Sensible precautions

- Levels of violent crime are relatively low but there are areas to avoid, as in every city. Places to avoid at night include the backstreet and dockside areas of Leith, wynds (narrow lanes) off the Royal Mile, the footpaths across the Meadows and other unlit urban areas.
- Scottish police officers wear a peaked flat hat with black-and-white chequered band and are friendly and approachable.
- Petty theft is the most common problem, so don't carry more cash than you need and beware of pickpockets, especially in the main tourist areas and on public transport. Take care of bags and do not leave them on backs of chairs.

## LANGUAGE

- There are many words that are uniquely Scottish and used in everyday conversation. Here are a few:

**auld** old
**awfy** very
**aye/naw** yes/no
**blether** to chatter, gossip
**bonnie** pretty, attractive
**braw** fine; good
**ceilidh** party or dance
**dram** a measure of whisky
**drouth/drouthy** thirst, thirsty
**gloaming** dusk
**ken** to know
**kirk** church
**laddie/lassie** boy/girl
**stravaig** wander; out on the town

# Index

# CityPack
## Edinburgh *Top 25*

**WRITTEN BY** Jackie Staddon and Hilary Weston
**CONTRIBUTIONS TO LIVING EDINBURGH** Sally Roy

A CIP catalogue record for this book is available from the British Library.

**ISBN-10:** 0-7495-4746-4
**ISBN-13:** 978-0-7495-4746-2

Published by AA Publishing, a trading name of Automobile Association Developments Limited, whose registered office is Fanum House, Basing View, Basingstoke, RG21 4EA. Registered number 1878835.

© **AUTOMOBILE ASSOCIATION DEVELOPMENTS LIMITED 2006**
First published January 2006. Reprinted Feb 2007

Colour separation by Keenes, Andover, UK
Printed and bound by Hang Tai D&P Limited, Hong Kong

**ACKNOWLEDGEMENTS**
The Automobile Association would like to thank the following photographers, libraries and agencies for their assistance in the preparation of this book.
Brand X Pictures back cover nightclub; Courtesy of Edinburgh Zoo 26t, 26b; Adam Elder, Scottish Parliament Photograph © 2005 Scottish Parliamentary Corporate Body 45; © Keith Hunter Photography 27, 34b, 56; © Our Dynamic Earth 46t, 46b; © The Royal Yacht Britannia 40t, 40b; Scotch Whisky Heritage Centre 33t; Stockbyte 4t; © The Trustees of the National Museums of Scotland 39b; The remaining images are held in the Association's own library (AA WORLD TRAVEL LIBRARY) and were taken by the following photographers:
Marius Alexander 21, 57t; Jim Carnie front cover, flag; Douglas Corrance front cover, Calton Hill, Camera Obscura, 1t, 2t, 3t, 6t, 9br, 11tl, 31, 36t, 43b, 49b, 59t, 89; Richard Elliott front cover, Scots Monument, 24cr, 48b; Isla Love 23; Ken Paterson front cover, Greyfriar's Bobby, piper, back cover, tartan, café, 8tl, 8tc, 8br, 9cr, 9bl, 11tr, 11bl, 12cl, 12b, 13, 14cr, 15tl, 25t, 28t, 29t, 29b, 30b, 32c, 33b, 34t, 36b, 37t, 38t, 38b, 39t, 41, 42t, 42b, 43t, 44t, 47t, 50; 51b, 52b, 53, 55t, 55b, 57bl, 57br, 58, 61t, 61b; Jonathan Smith front cover, fountain, back cover, castle, 7tl, 7tr, 8bl, 8cl, 9cl, 11br, 16cl, 19, 20b, 22b, 24cl, 30t, 32b, 35b, 37b, 44b, 48t, 49t, 51t, 52t, 54, 59b, 60, 62 and Stephen Whitehorne 9tr, 10tl, 12tl, 14tl, 14cl, 16tl, 18tl, 20tl, 22tl, 24tl, 25b, 35t.

**TITLES IN THE CITYPACK SERIES**
• Amsterdam • Bangkok • Barcelona • Beijing • Berlin • Boston • Brussels & Bruges • Chicago • • Dublin • Florence • Hong Kong • Istanbul • Las Vegas • Lisbon • London • Los Angeles • Madrid • Melbourne • Miami • Milan • Montréal • Munich • Naples • New York • Orlando • Paris • Prague • • Rome • San Francisco • Seattle • Shanghai • Singapore • Sydney • Tokyo • Toronto • Venice • • Vienna • Washington DC •